THE BRITISH AND IRISH IN OKLAHOMA

by Patrick J. Blessing

*Oklahoma Image is a project sponsored by the
Oklahoma Department of Libraries
and the Oklahoma Library Association,
and made possible by a grant from the
National Endowment for the Humanities.*

Library of Congress Cataloging in Publication Data

Blessing, Patrick J
  The British and Irish in Oklahoma.

(Newcomers to a new land)
Bibliography: p.
  1. British Americans—Oklahoma—History. 2. Irish Americans—Oklahoma—History. 3. Oklahoma—History. I. Title.
II. Series.
F705.B7B55   976.6'004'21   79-6722
ISBN 0-8061-1672-2

CONTENTS

To the Memory of Kate Barnard

PREFACE

Some of the terms used throughout this work require clarification. "British" is used in the sense that the English generally use it and the Americans generally accept it, to mean English, Scots and Welsh. I realize that the lesser partners in Great Britain—Scotland and Wales—are somewhat sensitive about this general usage, they carefully distinguish the political entity from the cultural divisions. Fortunately, such sensitivity has so far been absent from Oklahoma.

The Irish presented a different problem. To include them under the term "British" was to invite trouble. They are therefore simply called Irish. The term is meant to include immigrants from the Republic of Ireland and Northern Ireland. The "Irish" within Oklahoma are divided into four groups: immigrants born in Ireland, Oklahomans of Irish parentage, those whose grandparent or more distant ancestor was Irish, and individuals with Irish names who consider themselves "Irish" and yet have no discernible ancestor from the Green Isle. This study is confined to the first two of these groups.

When used for the period before 1890, the term "Oklahoma" means the area which later became the State of Oklahoma. The Organic Act of May 2, 1890, established the Oklahoma Territory in the area west of the Indian Territory. "Twin Territories" therefore is used for the period 1890–1907 to describe the land later to become the State of Oklahoma.

Finally, space requirements limited the number of maps to two. To identify Oklahoma locations discussed herein the reader should consult John W. Morris and Edwin C. McReynolds, *Historical Atlas of Oklahoma*, 2nd Edition (Norman: University of Oklahoma Press, 1971).

A number of people at the University of Tulsa helped make this work possible. Professor William Settle generously shared his vast store of information on Oklahoma and took time out from his own research to read and comment on an earlier draft. Professor Thomas Buckley, History Department Chairman, provided criticism and administrative aid as needed at critical stages of its completion. John Sandman performed most of the boring task of coding the data on which the work is largely based. Claudia Ellingsworth did most of the vital and time-consuming computer work. Lacinda Casey drew the maps. Lastly and most importantly, Mary Schenck did her usual outstanding job of editing and typing a well-worn manuscript. To these individuals I am most grateful.

Patrick J. Blessing

University of Tulsa

Chapter 1
ORIGINS

The caravans of settlers, having crossed the Cherokee strip to the northern boundary of Oklahoma, are spreading for miles along the boundary line . . . Noon tomorrow will witness a mad rush from all sides on fleet ponies to take the choicest lands, as the first comers will secure the first rights to the homesteads.

Thus on April 22, 1889, the *Times* of London announced the first of the "runs" which began mass white settlement of Oklahoma. The report, read widely throughout Britain and Ireland, had no discernible impact. Cross-Atlantic movement from these two areas had been underway for centuries and most of Oklahoma's white inhabitants had at least one British or Irish ancestor. Intermarriage between British or Irish newcomers and Indians during colonial days had produced the majority of "mixed-bloods" in many tribes forcibly moved by the United States government to Oklahoma in the nineteenth century. Immigrants from England, Ireland, Scotland, and Wales were well represented among settlers who began arriving in Oklahoma after the Civil War. They played an important role in the establishment and development of the most vital industry in the Sooner State: coal mining. Trade unions were introduced to Oklahoma by British and Irish workers. Most of the progressive clauses in the state's constitution were inserted through the political efforts of these enterprising northeastern Europeans. The Great Depression represented an important turning point for the English, Irish, Scots, and Welsh in Oklahoma, who were much weaker after the unprecedented economic collapse than before. Although they never regained their old importance, British and Irish newcomers and their descendants have made important contributions to the Sooner State in recent decades.

For most Oklahoma families the search for immigrant ancestors leads back to the craggy hills of New England, the tidewater of Virginia, or the fertile piedmont areas of the southern colonies. The principal ports in the colonies, Boston, New York, Philadelphia, Baltimore, and Charlestown, served as funnels to direct immigrant traffic to the interior. By the time of the American Revolution much of the fertile land east of the Appalachian Mountains was occupied. Some 92 percent of the population at that time were of British or Irish extraction. Beginning in the 1790s the population burst the banks of the Appalachian barrier moving in three great waves over old Indian trails that were widened into wagon roads (See Figure 1). The first and earliest wave extended from the middle colonies through the Cumberland Gap into areas that became Kentucky, Tennessee, and Missouri. The southernmost stream, which reached full flow after the Louisiana Purchase of 1803, stretched from the South Atlantic seaboard states down the Federal Road that rounded the southernmost ridge of the mountains and across the present states of Georgia, Alabama, Mississippi, and Arkansas. The northern stream stretched from New England and upstate New York across the Great Trail and National Road into the future states of Ohio, Indiana, Illinois, and Missouri. Most settlers in the Twin Territories after 1889 moved relatively short distances to the area, generally from adjacent states. To get to these jumping-off points most of their forebears had traveled along one of the two major southern streams of migration; the northern route was least popular. But regardless of their ancestors' particular route of migration, when Oklahomans extended the search for roots back to the immigrant generation they were usually of British or Irish ancestry.

The Indian population of Oklahoma can trace most of its mixed–blood members back to the British or Irish. Beginning in mid-eighteenth century, traders and ministers from England, Scotland, and Ireland fanned out among the native tribes in frontier areas of Pennsylvania and colonies farther south. Many intermarried with the Indians, in some cases because of the shortage of white women in frontier areas; in others, because it was much easier to do business or to convert a tribe when one acquired citizenship through marriage. After removal of the tribes to the Oklahoma area the descendants of "intermarried" British and Irish became part of a powerful mixblood faction. With the assistance of some more modern fullblood tribesmen, these mixblood families dominated tribal life, particularly in four of the five civilized tribes. Among the Cherokees, mixbloods of English and Scottish ancestry are still prominent: Rogers, Ward,

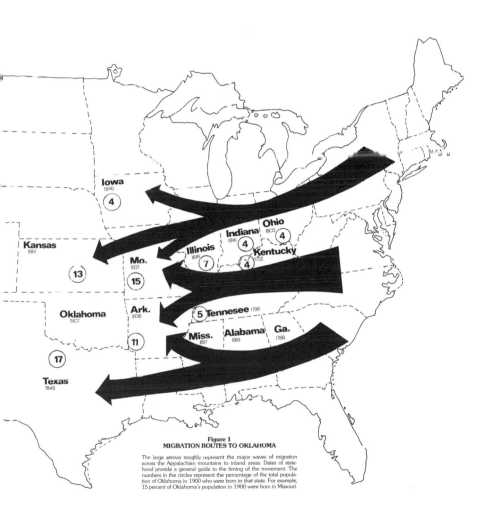

Figure 1
MIGRATION ROUTES TO OKLAHOMA

The large arrows roughly represent the major waves of migration across the Appalachian mountains to inland areas. Dates of statehood provide a general guide to the timing of the movement. The numbers in the circles represent the percentage of the total population of Oklahoma in 1900 who were born in that state. For example, 15 percent of Oklahoma's population in 1900 were born in Missouri.

The British and Irish in Oklahoma

Lowry, Reese, Hicks, Adair, Duncan, and Musgrove. Among the Creeks, the McIntosh, Stidham, McGillivray, and Grayson families dominated. The Chickasaws had the families of Colbert, Adair, Gunn, McGee, Allen, Harris, McLaughlin, Love, and McGillivray. Finally the Choctaws had the McKenney, Walker, Perry, Jones, and Locke families, and the McCurtains for whom a county in Oklahoma was named.

The settlement of the Twin Territories in the late nineteenth century coincided with peak periods of English, Scottish, and Welsh movement across the Atlantic and with impressive Irish immigration. Yet few newly arriving immigrants headed directly for the area. Only about 1 in 550 Scots, 1 in 770 Welsh, 1 in 1,000 English, and 1 in 3,600 Irish arriving in the United States between 1899 and 1910 declared Oklahoma as their destination. The majority of British and Irish arriving in Oklahoma during the runs had resided in the United States for some time. Despite the lack of interest in the Twin Territories as a destination among newly arriving British and Irish, these groups outnumbered all other foreign-born listed in the area on the federal censuses of 1890 and 1900. British and Irish immigrants to Oklahoma were as close to the cutting edge of settlement on the "last frontier" as any other immigrants.

The impressive cross-Atlantic movement from Britain and Ireland was spurred by conditions in the home society. Until well into the twentieth century, Ireland, England, Scotland, and Wales were sharply divided, geographically and socially. In England, the quiet traditional life of the more remote areas like Cornwall stood in stark contrast to the panic and poverty of Manchester and other industrial cities. Tenants on highland farms seemed centuries removed from the progressive residents of Lowland Scotland. Mountain dwellers of Wales had great difficulty adjusting to life in the industrialized coal-producing lowlands. The inhabitants of the more modern coastal cities and towns in the north and east of Ireland had little in common with peasants of the Gaelic-speaking west. The characteristics of emigrants from the two vastly different areas in each country tended to cancel each other out and made it difficult to generalize accurately about out-migration on a national level. Departures were also a reaction to differing unknown local conditions. Yet it is essential to examine the background; immigrant success or failure in America was closely related to the experience in the homeland.

Some common features underlay British and Irish migration across the Atlantic. The movement was part of a great dispersal of

4

European peoples to all parts of the world. An impressive increase in population touched all four countries after mid-eighteenth century. A rapid rise in the level of trans-Atlantic commerce followed the end of the Napoleonic Wars in 1815 and spurred a drive by shipping agents to encourage emigrants to travel to the United States as fare-paying passengers on ships that would have otherwise have gone back in ballast. Over the same years knowledge of the world outside of areas of birth became widespread among inhabitants of each country. This was the direct outcome of rising literacy because of the establishment of public schools. Thus population pressure, the increasing availability of shipping, and growing knowledge of the United States combined with local conditions to dictate the tempo and composition of emigration from England, Ireland, Scotland, and Wales.

The transformation of the pre-industrial economic order in England, involving the emergence of a national state, the enclosure of lands, and the industrialization of the society was accompanied by significant movement of population out of the country. A few departed because of religious intolerance, usually in the early years, but the majority left for economic reasons. After a number of unsuccessful efforts to colonize North America by the English, the first settlement was established at Jamestown in 1607. This was followed by the Pilgrim landing at Plymouth and the establishment of the Massachusetts Bay Colony by the New England Company. The Middle Colonies were first settled by New Jersey colonists in the 1660s, by the acquisition of New York in 1667, and by the Quaker migration to Pennsylvania in the 1680s. English entry into the Carolinas began with the Albemarle colony (later North Carolina) in 1670. In the early eighteenth century English settlements were established in South Carolina, Georgia, and Maryland. Initially English colonial settlers were generally of relatively high social status in the home society, from the middle rungs or above on the social ladder. But in later years a significant number came from the bottom of society, such as convicts, paupers, and laborers. To earn their passage to the Colonies poorer travelers usually sold themselves as indentured servants or redemptioners into several years of serfdom.

The modernization of England became more intense during the nineteenth century. The consolidation of land continued, the population expanded, and industrialization became more widespread. Rural dwellers found it increasingly difficult to make a living and many headed for England's industrial cities. But city dwellers also had their anxieties; almost every decade saw an intense economic downturn.

5

As a result emigration spread to all levels of society. Movement out of England took place in a series of waves, each more powerful than its predecessor. By 1850 about one in twenty emigrants were farmers, one-third were laborers, the remainder were artisans or skilled industrial workers. The proportion of unskilled workers decreased gradually towards the end of the century. Overall, throughout the nineteenth century the great majority of English emigrants were well prepared by their industrial skills and experiences in a modern society for life in the United States. In absolute numbers the English immigration reached a peak in 1911, shortly after the declaration of Oklahoma's statehood.

Welsh migration to the American colonies was relatively insignificant. A few Welsh names appear on lists of indentured servants. Some Quakers, Baptists, and Presbyterians, fleeing persecution and poverty, also left Wales for Colonial America. The most prominent Welsh settlement in the colonies was founded by Quaker Richard Davies on 5,000 acres of Pennsylvania land purchased from William Penn. The Methodist revival in mid-eighteenth century Wales inspired many Welsh missionaries to head for back-country settlements on the American frontier. By the time of the American Revolution a number of books in Welsh were being published in the colonies and a Welsh society had been founded in Philadelphia for the relief of destitute newcomers.

Officials did not distinguish between newcomers from England and Wales over the nineteenth century. But obviously there was impressive movement from Wales to the United States in the early decades for by 1820 Welsh communities had sprouted in Pennsylvania, New York, and Ohio. Between 1815 and 1850 most Welsh emigrants came from rural areas, driven from the homeland by agrarian discontent and attracted to the New World by the availability of large amounts of cheap land. About half of all Welsh immigrants after mid-century were skilled workers; only about one in 10 were farmers. Among the skilled workers were a great many miners, particularly after 1880 when Welsh mines went into decline. The all-time peak in numbers of Welsh moving to the United States was in 1890.

The transformation of the old economic and social order in Scotland began in the late seventeenth century and involved the consolidation of joint holdings of land into single farms. The changes in rural social relationships which resulted were intensified by rapid population growth. Although some Scots moved to the American colonies as early as 1650, not until the early 1700s did large-scale movement across the Atlantic begin. By the time of the American Revolution, Scottish merchants were well established in all colonial ports. Artisans and laborers from the Lowlands had been arriving for decades in New York and Virginia. Many Highlanders had arrived: some as indentured servants, others in groups under minor chiefs. Significant numbers of these traditional mountaineers appeared in frontier areas from New York to as far south as Georgia.

From the American Revolution to 1875, Scottish migration to the United States remained slow but steady. During the last quarter of the nineteenth century, however, a decline in demand for rural labor in Scotland led to a significant increase in cross-Atlantic traffic. Industrial decline in the early twentieth century, particularly after World War I, expanded this stream. Scottish immigrants, at least 50 percent in skilled occupations, included a large representation of professionals, teachers, merchants, and doctors. The volume of movement across the Atlantic from Scotland during the 1920s was unprecedented and the number of Scots in the United States peaked in 1930, far later than for any other British group or the Irish.

Given Ireland's long tradition of internal migration and her strategic location as the final provisioning point on the long journey from England to the American colonies, it was inevitable that many Irish eventually left for the New World. The first significant migration was spurred by economic problems and religious discrimination directed at one time or another against all major religions. In the seventeenth century Catholic emigrants left in large numbers as bonded servants, convicts, or prisoners of war. But there was also a small but powerful element of affluent Irish Catholic emigrants. By the time of the American Revolution there was a Catholic Irish presence in all major American cities, particularly Philadelphia.

The most numerous emigrants from Ireland, and to Oklahomans the best known, are the "Scotch-Irish," Presbyterian descendants of Scottish settlers who colonized the northern counties of Ireland in the early seventeenth century. Although some of them moved to the American colonies as early as 1680, mass Presbyterian movement across the Atlantic did not start until 1718. Most Irish Presbyterians went to the Middle Colonies, particularly Pennsylvania, where they came to comprise almost a quarter of the population by the time of the American Revolution. By 1800 Presbyterians had dominated movement from Ireland for almost a century and were scattered throughout the fledgling American states, particularly in frontier areas. Irish Episcopalians and Irish Quakers blended into the colonies

7

with a minimum of friction. Many Episcopalians came as indentured servants, particularly to Virginia, but also to Georgia and the Carolinas. A few of the more affluent remained in urban areas where they prospered. The majority of Irish Quakers moved to Pennsylvania where they joined communities of fellow Quakers from the British Isles. Their descendants eventually moved into the Shenandoah Valley of Virginia and farther south. By the Revolution, there were "Friends" and Episcopalians of Irish birth or descent in Pennsylvania, Delaware, Virginia, South Carolina, and Georgia.

The economic downturn in Ireland that followed the end of the Napoleonic Wars in 1815, and continued population growth combined to make life increasingly difficult for many in rural Ireland, particularly on the lower levels. Unfortunately, there was little industrial development to absorb the energies of the expanding population. The only alternative to starvation was emigration. From 1815 to the first year of the Great Famine, 1845, over 1.3 million Irish left the homeland. The famine intensified these trends, and a high level of departures continued almost up to the 1960s. Movement out of the country peaked in 1849, far earlier than for other countries of the British Isles. The Irish-born population in the United States was at its largest in the census of 1890, on the eve of massive white settlement of Oklahoma.

Irish emigration underwent significant changes during the nineteenth century. Until the mid-1830s, most Irish emigrants were Protestants who traveled to the United States via Canada because of the cheaper fares to America's northern neighbor. After 1840, however, impoverished Catholics from a rural background who generally traveled directly to the United States made up the bulk of Irish migrating across the Atlantic Ocean. From the Great Famine to the mid-twentieth century about four out of five of all Irish emigrants held unskilled rural occupations at home; the remaining one in five were professionals, traders, artisans, and managers. Overall, Ireland unwittingly exported her poor, losing a larger proportion of her population in the effort than any other country in Europe.

Some British immigrants left the homeland during colonial years inspired by the hope that they could revive in the New World a society which they felt was rapidly decaying at home. The Puritans wanted to recreate a traditional religious community. A few Scottish highland chiefs tried to save the disintegrating clan system by transplanting it to the American colonies. But most cross-Atlantic migrants had more immediate and modest goals, particularly in the nineteenth century.

The uncertainty of the future rather than actual poverty encouraged most departures from England, Scotland, and Wales. For the great majority of Irish, poverty provided the spur. They were leaving because, as they sang, in America there was "bread and work for all and the sun shines always there."

Few British or Irish emigrants tackled the Atlantic alone: kinship networks generally facilitated the movement. Many, in some years a majority, moved in family groups, mother and father together with their children. Those not moving in a primary family group invariably shared surnames with at least one fellow passenger, suggesting a blood relationship, or traveled with individuals from similar areas of origin. The role of relatives in raising the funds to pay passage further underscored the importance of group action in facilitating the migration. Frequently individuals at home or in the New World pooled resources to aid in the movement of relatives. This was particularly true of the Irish, most of whom from the 1840s to the early years of the twentieth century paid their fares with the aid of relatives.

An immigrant's destination in the New World was determined by the availability of jobs and the location of friends or relatives. Generally in the early years both of these coincided: it was friends or relatives from home who found the newcomer a job and provided aid in adjusting to the shock of arrival. As the years passed in the United States, however, an immigrant became increasingly likely to move for economic reasons. Some skilled British industrial workers—coal miners, hard-rock Cornish miners, Welsh iron workers—traveled along fixed routes to jobs in all areas of the United States, from Pittsburgh to the mines of Illinois or California. Coal miners in this stream frequently ended up in the Indian Territory. But this attachment to a particular occupation was unusual. The great majority of British and Irish newcomers moved through a variety of jobs as they drifted from place to place across the United States.

Although individual English, Welsh, and Lowland Scots generally felt some sense of alienation for a period after arrival, from earliest days these groups blended easily into American society. Difference in dress and behavior made adjustment more difficult for Highland Scots and Irish. For the former this was a problem only during early colonial days, for modernization of the homeland changed forever the way of life of Highlanders by the time of the American Revolution. The Irish had a different experience.

In contrast to the predominantly Presbyterian Irish from more modern areas of the homeland, who blended into American society without friction, the generally impoverished Catholic Irish made a slow and painful adjustment. The antipathy in colonial times towards Catholics, expressed in widespread discriminatory legislation, continued into the nineteenth century and inspired the Know-Nothing anti-Catholicism of the 1840s. Around this time, Irish Presbyterians and their descendants assumed widespread use of the designation "Scotch-Irish" to disassociate themselves from impoverished Catholic countrymen. This same impulse to avoid identification as Catholic led many Sons of Erin to change their names to ones not readily identifiable as Hibernian. Some also changed their religion. Impressive Irish-Catholic participation in the Civil War won them grudging respect. This feeling of goodwill was intensified by the work of "accommodationists." These writers, politicians, and intellectuals, both immigrant and native, labored to lower the barriers between the Irish and the larger society. By 1900, Irish Catholics were an accepted element in the American social mosaic and to most Americans Saint Patrick's Day was a community holiday as well as an Irish festival. Thus the mass white settlement of Oklahoma began at a time when the English, Welsh, Scots, and Irish were well accepted in American society.

Chapter 2

PRE-STATEHOOD

Oklahoma, like the Eternal City, was not built in a day. The settlement of the area by whites, including British and Irish newcomers, began hesitantly in the early nineteenth-century. Dublin-born Alexandro O'Reilly, based in New Orleans, was one of the last governors of the Spanish Territory which included Oklahoma before the region was acquired by France and then by the United States in 1803 through the Louisiana Purchase. Trappers of British and Irish ancestry were among the first Americans to operate in Oklahoma. Fur traders Benjamin Murphy, Hugh Love, and Hugh Glenn ranged the Oklahoma area in the early decades of the nineteenth century. Daring trapper Alex McFarland was killed by an Osage war party in 1812. World-renowned English naturalist, Thomas Nuttall, spent several months in 1819 collecting botanical specimens in eastern Oklahoma. Two Irishmen, Nolan and Myers, among a group of explorers led by a United States Army Major Long which included Thomas Say, noted pioneer zoologist, distinguished themselves by deserting the poorly-led expedition in 1820. As the largest immigrant group in the United States Army during the nineteenth century, many Irish served in the chain of military posts that were built across Oklahoma, beginning in 1824 with Fort Gibson.

Migration of British and Irish to the Oklahoma area gathered momentum after the Civil War. Scottish entrepreneurs operated cattle companies, including the Cattle Ranche and Land Company, that leased sizeable range rights in Indian Territory and No Man's Land in the Oklahoma Panhandle. Poor business decisions and disagreements over sale of land rights to outsiders resulted in substantial losses for their investors. Irish laborers worked on the Missouri, Kansas and Texas railroad between McAlester, Indian Territory, and Denison, Texas, in 1872; others labored as tracklayers in the northern

11

areas of Indian Territory. A handful of these sturdy Sons of Erin remained after the railroad crews moved on: two lie buried in the Atoka church graveyard. Only one Irish railroad worker is remembered.

Pat Shanahan was a dependable man. He came to Cherokee country as a section foreman for the Atlantic and Pacific Railroad. As the tracklayers neared the present-day town of Vinita, Shanahan had a disagreement with the company and was fired. Believing that he had been treated unfairly, he set out to even the score. Shanahan married a young Cherokee woman he had known for some time and thus became a citizen of the tribe. Every tribal member was authorized to lay claim to as much land as he could farm, and Shanahan selected a piece of property at the end of the railroad track. When the company decided to resume building, they discovered Shanahan's barn directly across the route of the track. "Shanahan's War" ensued. At first the railroad company tried to move Shanahan by force, to no avail. Then they resorted to legal action rightly claiming that the land had been set aside by congressional action for railroad building. Shanahan stood fast on his rights as a Cherokee citizen and again prepared to defend himself. The company was eventually forced to agree to Shanahan's terms; he was paid handsomely to vacate his land.

This process of whites becoming citizens of Indian tribes through intermarriage was widespread throughout the nineteenth century, vastly expanding the number of intermarried tribal members and eventually the number of mixed-bloods. Long before the run of 1889, intermarriage with Indians became an accepted avenue of advancement for whites in Indian Territory. Kilkenny-born Benedictine Brother John Laracy was walking along a roadway near Atoka in 1879 when he encountered an old white farmer who inquired as to who he was. Brother John, apparently reluctant to identify himself as a Catholic cleric, answered that he had come to the area to seek his fortune. "Find a good-looking Indian woman and your fortune is made," advised the farmer. Many British and Irish immigrants and native whites took this marital route to riches, thus acquiring access to Indian lands and resources, initially coal, later oil.

By the time of the Civil War prominent mixed-bloods of British background controlled a great deal of the land in Indian Territory which they worked with slave labor. Joseph Vann of the Cherokee Nation, David McIntosh of the Creeks, and Robert Love of the Chickasaws were among the wealthiest cotton growers in Indian

Territory. After the Civil War they resumed activities with the aid of contract labor. Towards the end of the nineteenth century constant in-migration of native whites, including some of British or Irish birth or ancestry, rapidly expanded the numbers of intermarried tribal members. Irishman Theodore Fitzpatrick came to the United States at eighteen years of age and, after a period in Boston, headed for the Choctaw Nation where he married a part-Choctaw woman, thereby acquiring rights to land. By the 1890s he occupied a 1500 acre farm near the present town of Bradley, Oklahoma. All the major tribes had very powerful intermarried whites whose wealth was based on their access to Indian land. Some tribes, like the Seminoles and Osages had a relatively small number of mixed-bloods. Others, like the Chickasaws had so many that fullblood members of the tribe were in a distinct minority. The impressive level of interaction between British and Irish newcomers, their descendants, and others in the society, both white and Indian, underscores the hazards of any rigid identification of Oklahomans as members of a single ethnic group.

Life changed markedly for all inhabitants of the Oklahoma area in 1889. At noon on April 22 of that year, on the borders of the Unassigned Lands in the center of the present-day state, a United States Army bugler signaled the opening of land to white settlers. Among the thousands who staked out claims in the ensuing mad scramble were 756 British and Irish. Most attempted to settle farms; a few tried their luck in areas they hoped would become booming towns. Guthrie was the town location most favored by these newcomers, Oklahoma City was a close second. By 1900, the number of British and Irish newcomers in the Twin Territories had expanded to 4,290 with the English leading, followed by Irish, Scots, and Welsh. At the same time, the population with British or Irish parentage numbered over 10,000, the largest group of any foreign background in the territories that became the State of Oklahoma.

Few newcomers from Great Britain and Ireland traveled directly to the Twin Territories. The places of birth recorded for their children revealed the broad outline of their routes of migration. The typical homesteader had previously resided in at least three states. Most had failed as farmers a number of times and had taken temporary non-farm employment to survive. But they never forgot the dream of land ownership, and it eventually led them to the Twin Territories. While routes of migration were roughly similar to those of other settlers, there was a slight tendency for British and Irish immigrants to travel greater distances to the Oklahoma area, perhaps indicating a greater sensitivity to opportunities for economic advancement.

Between the time of the first land run in 1889 and the announcement of statehood in 1907, British and Irish settlers in Oklahoma shared distinct characteristics. They were generally older than other white residents: two out of three were over forty years of age. About 80 percent of the Welsh and Scots and 60 percent of the English and Irish were married, frequently to someone of a different nationality. Four out of five English and Scots newcomers and one out of four Irish and Welsh married outside of their group. On the average, British and Irish newcomers had been in the United States an incredible thirty years prior to arrival in the area. Rates of naturalization varied between groups. The Irish led with 80 percent having gone through the process; next in importance came the English, Scots, and Welsh.

Life for these immigrant settlers was tough. In the early years they lived in tents, sod huts or makeshift houses built of local materials. They worried about crops, weather, money, and most of all about their children who died at an alarming rate. After a hard day's labor in the fields, English homesteader John Eggleston returned to his sod house north of Guthrie in the fall of 1899. His wife Mary was trying to take care of their only child, a three-year-old boy who was apparently suffering from a respiratory ailment. During the night the lad died. The neighbors came and assisted as best they could with the burial. For weeks afterward Mary Eggleston sat at the window of the cabin looking out across the bleak prairie in the direction of the graveyard. Death touched the majority of British and Irish settlers in this manner; more than half of them had children die at birth or in the early years of life. Occasionally one of the parents died, particularly among the Irish, who had the largest proportion of widows and widowers—about one in ten of all family heads. Yet the optimism that had kept them going during the hardships of the long trek to the Twin Territories eventually returned. Mary Eggleston came out of her "blues," as the neighbors called it, and had another child the following summer. Then the family moved on, as did a great many others of the original settlers. Most moved out because they failed. Some simply gave up because of the loneliness and uncertainty of settler life. Still others saw better opportunity elsewhere.

Community life for British and Irish homesteaders differed little from that of other settlers. They visited back and forth regularly with their neighbors. Frequently a few settlers would get together and hold a country dance. These were quiet affairs, with little drinking or

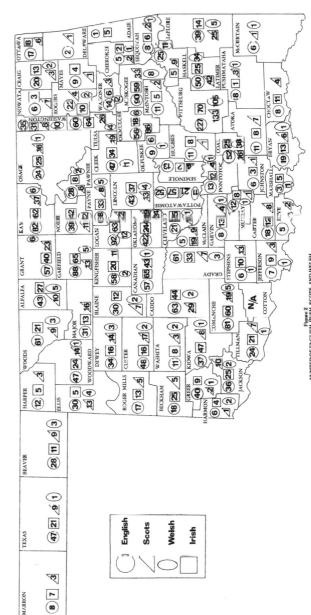

Figure 2
NUMBER OF ENGLISH, IRISH, SCOTS, AND WELSH
IN OKLAHOMA'S COUNTIES IN 1910.

carousing, where all made a great effort to appear friendly and happy. Literary societies organized singing, recitation, and debating meetings in individual homes. Various lodges attracted members from across a wide swath of the prairie. Political rallies and medicine shows provided further relief from the drab routine of life on a farm. The Fourth of July, Thanksgiving, and Christmas provided opportunities for major community celebrations. Settlers on isolated claims a long distance from town generally stayed overnight to attend festivals and rarely experienced any difficulty in finding a place to stay without charge. Despite the competitiveness of the various land runs, the Oklahoma countryside was a neighborly place where people were united by common challenges. Given the similarities in the backgrounds of all settlers prior to arrival in the Twin Territories, it was a rare British or Irish immigrant who talked with a native-born neighbor for any length of time without finding that they shared common experiences.

Although some English, Scots, Welsh, and Irish came as individuals, the majority arrived in the Twin Territories in family units. Only a few Irish attempted to form communities of their own. After settling in tiny Edgewood in Chickasaw country in 1875 Frank Murray changed the name of the community to Erin Springs in honor of his homeland and tried to attract other Irish. He was arrested in 1901 by tribal police for having eight white tenants on his farm in violation of Chickasaw law. Spurning the high-priced services of "Alfalfa Bill" Murray—the future governor—as his defense lawyer, he bought a jug of whiskey for the jury which they freely consumed during his trial. He was acquitted. In the early 1890s groups of Irish settled in a few townships, for example, Hennessey in Kingfisher County or Deer Creek in Oklahoma County, both of which acquired reputations as "Irish towns." But in less than a decade more than 90 percent of the original Irish settler families in both communities had moved and were replaced by native-born newcomers. These places represented the most successful efforts by any of four groups to establish ethnic communities.

Recruitment of miners for Indian Territory coalfields began in 1873 in Pennsylvania. The pioneer British and Irish miners who answered that call established the coal industry and many of the present-day communities in the southeast regions of Oklahoma. On a harsh winter's day in 1880 a group of Welsh immigrants, after failing as farmers in a settlement in New Philadelphia, Texas, arrived in Indian Territory to attempt mining. As railroads were built the market for coal expanded and the industry grew steadily for several decades. Over the same period recruiters shifted their activities to mining areas throughout the entire United States. The typical immigrant in the mines had been away from home more than 20 years and had labored in a number of coalfields throughout the United States before being attracted to the Indian Territory by high wages and steady work. Skilled British and Irish miners were far less likely than non-miners to have worked previously outside of their major occupation. While the proportion of British and Irish newcomers in the general mining population dropped off in the late 1890s, for most of the territorial years the majority of miners were of British and Irish birth or parentage.

Labor conditions for miners in the Oklahoma area were the most dangerous in the United States. Not until well into the twentieth century was labor-saving machinery introduced. Almost all mining in the early days was done with hand tools by individuals who sometimes worked an entire shift on their knees or in awkward stooped positions, more often than not in water several inches deep. Lack of ventilation was a serious problem and combined with the haphazard use of explosives to produce "windy shots"—dust explosions—which killed many miners. The tribal government ignored this situation. Little was done to improve conditions until a Krebs mine explosion killed ninety-six men in 1892 and crippled over twice that number. The United States government stepped in and appointed an inspector of mines for Indian Territory. A marked improvement was noted immediately in mine safety.

But safety problems were far from solved. British and Irish miners appeared regularly among the lists of victims of mining accidents compiled by the federal mine inspector. On January 20, 1879, a young Irish miner, Pat Kairns, was struck by a piece of loose slate which fell from the roof of the mine in which he was working. He died shortly thereafter leaving a wife and two small children. The management claimed that Kairns was warned by his working partner that the roof was unsafe but replied, "I am not afraid." When Scottish-born Charles Ranken was widening a coal face on March 25, 1896, the roof fell and killed him. The superintendent claimed that he had been told to set up timbers to prevent such an accident. These accidents did not likely result from foolhardiness, as management claimed. The system compelled a miner to take risks. To qualify for the basic wage he had to send a certain amount of coal to the surface. A miner who stopped to investigate every time he suspected an unsafe condition simply could not keep his job. British ex-miners in management made significant contributions to mine safety. William Cameron, the Scottish-born superintendent of the Osage Coal and Mining Company in Krebs, developed an open-faced mining system which he installed over the objections of miners and federal safety inspectors. It proved a significant improvement over old mining techniques, reducing injuries and deaths associated with the industry in earlier days.

British and Irish miners with union experience became leaders in efforts to improve work conditions and wages. Local unions formed by these activists became part of District 21 of the United Mine Workers in 1890. By that time owners had formed an effective association which fought constantly to prevent concessions to labor and to erode gains made by miners in earlier days when labor was scarce. The severe strikes which resulted led to the deportation of many British and Irish from the Choctaw coal country by the United States Army after owners succeeded in getting reactionary tribal authorities to revoke the strikers' permission to stay in the area. Similarly, a strike in 1898 fell apart under determined pressure from the owners. But despite efforts to import blacks and "new" immigrants as strikebreakers, the northern Europeans prevailed. Led by Peter Hanraty, the Scottish-born president of District 21, the union grew from 400 to 16,000 members. Among British and Irish union miners who aided Hanraty in the battle with management were Jack Britton, P. R. Stewart, Jack O'Brien, Alex Howat, Andrew McGarry, and William Dalrymple. They achieved a major victory over management in 1903. Owners were forced to recognize the union, to accept the eight-hour workday, and to check-off union dues. The Agreement of 1903 was the most important document in labor relations in the coal mining industry in the Southwest.

Hanraty was also a founder and first president of the earliest and most important coalition of organized workers in the Oklahoma area. The Twin Territorial Federation of Labor, was established in 1903 by delegates from over fifty local unions. This organization had a profound impact on the politics of early Oklahoma, largely because of the stability and political skills of its immigrant leaders. It became an affiliate of the American Federation of Labor, very adept at living up to the dictum of the leader of the national organization, Samuel Gompers: "Elect labor's friends and defeat labor's enemies." Moreover, like Gompers, the leaders of the Twin Territorial Federation of Labor were relatively conservative in their definition of labor's friends. Although individual socialists of British background such as Patrick

Peter Hanraty. Courtesy of the Oklahoma Historical Society.

S. Nagle were popular among union members, the Socialists were generally rejected. Oklahoma's labor leaders were convinced that the radical group was of little value to the long-range interests of working men.

Most British and Irish miners were married and resided with their families. The household invariably consisted of the immediate family, rarely was there an older relative present as was the case of immigrant groups on the East Coast. Families were usually smaller and living conditions better for British and Irish miners than for others from southeast Europe. The high salaries that explain the better living conditions were a result of the higher skill level in northern Europe. Most British and Irish immigrants had extensive experience in the industry prior to arrival in Indian Territory, but most "new" immigrants were beginners in the industry. British and Irish miners generally owned their own homes; the Scots and English were more likely to own property than the Irish. All four groups sent their children, particularly the females, to school. Among children over sixteen years old in Irish families, one in five girls attended school but all boys labored in the mines. Few Irish or British wives worked as domestic servants despite a heavy demand for servants and maids, although on occasion they might take in boarders. Whenever a northern European woman engaged as a domestic servant it was invariably a daughter of a family in extremely poor circumstances.

The Socialist party first became powerful among British and Irish miners in Indian Territory during the "long strike" that ended in 1903. With the party's growing strength a leadership struggle developed among miners between Socialists under the direction of Scottish-born Alex Howat and less radical newcomers headed by Peter Hanraty. The war between the factions was fought on two fronts, labor organization and politics. Hanraty was generally a step ahead of the more radical element. In 1899 he was elected mayor of Coalgate. The first election victory of the Socialists was in 1904 when the party's candidate, Welsh miner John Ingram, was elected mayor of Krebs, and he managed to remain in office for two years. Socialist strength peaked in 1908 when District 21 of the United Mine Workers elected Alex Howat to replace Pete Hanraty as their leader. But Hanraty was not one to retire so easily; he ran successfully for mayor of McAlester. As mayor of the largest city in southeast Oklahoma and representative of the Catholic Democratic faction of the United Mine Workers, Hanraty provided miners with a political alternative to socialism until he was recalled by voters during the violent McAlester streetcar strike of 1912.

While owner efforts to reduce wages and break the union provided the primary impetus for Socialist activity in the mines during the early twentieth century, the activities of British and Irish organizers were very important in the development of the radical group. Welsh-born Alex Howat and John Ingram spoke at rallies all over southeast Oklahoma. But equally as important were organizers from outside of the state. By far the most popular of these was Mother Jones. This grandmotherly figure from County Cork, Ireland, weighing less than 100 pounds, was nationally known and admired for her fearlessness and persuasive speaking. From the Great Railroad Strike of 1877 until the late 1920s, she led strikes, went to jail frequently, and won the respect of the nation's miners. Her descriptions of life in company towns where police, judges, newspapers, and preachers conspired to exploit the miners, stirred the blood of miner and non-miner alike. It was an analysis which struck a chord of those attempting to cope with Oklahoma's reactionary owners. In 1906, she packed United Mine Worker union halls throughout Indian Territory.

Mother Jones was only one of many out-of-state organizers of Irish birth or parentage important in building support for socialism in Oklahoma. Irish-born Thomas "Red Tom" Hickey, editor of the Texas socialist newspaper, the *Rebel,* was a popular and inspirational speaker at labor and political rallies. Thomas J. Hagerty, an articulate and intelligent priest of Irish background from a parish in Las Vegas, New Mexico, became an effective organizer in Oklahoma and surrounding states. After a short three years of radical activity he was invited to join Mother Jones and other delegates in Chicago to launch the Industrial Workers of the World in 1906. Dan Hogan, a lawyer of Irish ancestry, based in Huntington, Arkansas, frequently lectured in support of socialist causes throughout eastern Oklahoma. Frank O'Hare, born in St. Louis of Irish parents, farmed near Vinita from 1905 to 1909 and served as Socialist party organizer for Indian Territory. He successfully predicted the support for the socialist cause among the "rack rented" farmers which was expressed in the 1912 presidential election.

Religion was an important part of the life of the native and immigrant population in early Oklahoma. The Methodists were the most prominent of a wide variety of Protestant denominations in the larger society, and their churches appeared in most communities after a few successful harvests. Welsh immigrants were almost universally Methodists, so their religious needs were most often met. English and Scottish immigrants from other Protestant denominations had little difficulty accepting the Methodist services until their church was built. There was even a certain amount of religious interaction among Protestants and Catholics. Many Irish-born Catholics attended Protestant churches, sometimes because of pressure from non-Catholic spouses or because of the absence of Catholic churches in a society where "respectable citizens" attended church. As a result many Irish members of the Roman Church changed their religion. Catholics from the Green Isle who retained their religion frequently traveled long distances on Sundays to attend mass. Some Catholic churches in the Twin Territories were built with the financial support of Protestant neighbors, usually businessmen. This ecumenical spirit did not last very long after statehood.

Catholic clergy of Irish and English birth or parentage were important in the Oklahoma area during the nineteenth century. Under the direction of two Irish bishops, Byrne and Fitzgerald of the Diocese of Little Rock, Arkansas, Father Peter Walsh wandered the Indian Territory during pre–Civil War days providing religious aid to scattered military posts, particularly to Irish soldiers. Ably assisting him were fellow clerics, John Monaghan and Patrick O'Reilly. One year after the end of the Civil War, the first of two famous Irish-born brothers, Father Laurence Smyth, began his activities, performing marriage ceremonies and baptisms at Fort Sill and other military posts. In 1868 he was joined by his younger brother, Michael, an enterprising priest who arranged with Irish railroad laborers and two local businessmen, John Hardin and John Dillon, to build Saint Patrick's Church at Atoka.

In addition to its role as the first Catholic church in Indian Territory, the Atoka church served for years as the center of Catholicism in Oklahoma. Father Isidore Robot used Saint Patrick's as his headquarters during his mid-1870s explorations to locate a site for a Benedictine monastery. The location of a suitable site in 1876 led to the founding of the Sacred Heart Mission which served as a Benedictine abbey until 1929, when the order moved their headquarters to Saint Gregory's in Shawnee. The Sacred Heart Mission attracted many Irish and English priests and brothers to the Twin Territories. Among them were English-born Brother Harding and Father Thomas Bergh, Brother John from County Kilkenny who distinguished himself by leaving a very useful memoir of life in Indian Territory, Irish-born Brother Patrick Phelan who labored hard and unsuccessfully to establish the mission of Saint Michael's, and an English-Irishman, Brother Columbus O'Loane, who found life in the Oklahoma area so unendurable that he departed after one year. Joining these foreign-born priests were a number of important Irish-Americans. Most notable was Father Bernard Murphy whose efforts as a builder of church edifices and schools rivaled the best "bricks and mortar" priest on the East Coast. He later had the misfortune of being elected abbot of his order in Oklahoma at a time when the group was rent with rivalries which he was never able to solve.

Among the factors cited by natives to explain the ready acceptance of English, Irish, Scottish, and Welsh newcomers were knowledge of English, ready adaptation of American customs, lack of tendency towards segregation, interest in political and civic affairs, intermarriage with natives, and permanent residence in the United States. The assimilation was evident in patterns of social interaction, particularly participation in fraternal organizations. British and Irish newcomers generally belonged to the same societies as the native whites. Their social mobility reflected this adjustment to the larger society. By 1907 many of the early arrivals from Britain and Ireland had become wealthy. In the mining areas many highly skilled jobs — supervisors, mine foremen, and engineers — were held by British or Irish or their children. Two Irishmen, James Degnan and James McConnell, owned one of the largest mines in the coal country, the McAlester Coal and Mineral Company. English-born Peter Coyne of Vinita started out as a homesteader. He then became a successful lawyer and eventually was elected a member of the house of representatives and senate in the new state. John J. Burke from Scotland had arrived in Oklahoma City in 1889 and within ten years bought out the *Norman Transcript* and became its editor.

The best known "Irishman" in Oklahoma was second generation Dennis T. Flynn. Born at Phoenixville, Pennsylvania, in 1861, Flynn was the son of a County Cork refugee from the Great Famine. Both parents died when he was three and Flynn grew up in a Catholic orphanage in Buffalo, New York. While a young man he moved throughout the Midwest and West working as a printer, newspaperman, politician, homesteader, and town speculator before finally being admitted to the bar in Kansas. He arrived in Guthrie on April 22, 1889, the first day of the run, to serve as postmaster. The recognition of his political talent by the Republican party resulted in nomination as a delegate from the Territory. He easily won the election.

Dennis Flynn's success in politics was based on a talent for impressing voters with his concern for their welfare. A quiet, courteous man who genuinely liked people, he never failed to talk to children and kiss the grubbiest babies in an audience. An indefatigable worker, Flynn traversed the territory speaking sometimes in several towns on the same day. To early Oklahomans he came across not as one of the celluloid-collar heroes who turned up to promise the moon before every election but as one of themselves. He won the hearts of listeners naturally suspicious of his Republicanism and Catholicism, some of whom greeted the opening of his speeches with jeers. But when he talked of the perils of farming and frontier life, the crowds grew silent. Here was someone who knew the terrors of prairie weather, the fear of uncontrollable market conditions, the threat of the overhanging mortgage, the dreams for the children, and the necessity for peace and order throughout the countryside. In the opinion of oldtimers, he was the most effective campaigner ever to appear in Oklahoma politics.

In Washington Flynn distinguished himself by securing passage of a number of very important bills, although territorial delegates had no vote in Congress. He worked hard on behalf of homesteaders and secured passage of the Free Homes Bill, providing free land to settlers on a number of newly opened Indian reservations. The bill saved impoverished farmers about $15 million. Equally important was Flynn's sponsorship of the "piecemeal absorption" plan for statehood. Introduced on January 3, 1896, the bill called for the immediate admission of Oklahoma Territory to the Union and the gradual annexation of Indian Territory as its areas prepared for statehood. Although defeated, the bill spurred interest and planning for eventual statehood. Retiring from politics in 1902, Flynn embarked on a very successful legal career. As politician and businessman, Dennis Flynn had few equals among leading Oklahoma pioneers.

On the land, in the mines, or in the towns, these immigrant pioneers were a sturdy hard-case lot, for whom the American dream of rags to riches meant much. Arriving with little money, nothing was given them save in a few cases, the land. Their primary assets were optimism, endurance and confidence in themselves. Throughout their lives, many, perhaps most, failed, and in a few places the ruins of their deserted cabins still dot the Oklahoma prairie. The sufferings and sacrifices of those who disappeared, who come closer to representing the "typical settler" than the successful ones, remain the great untold story of the American experience.

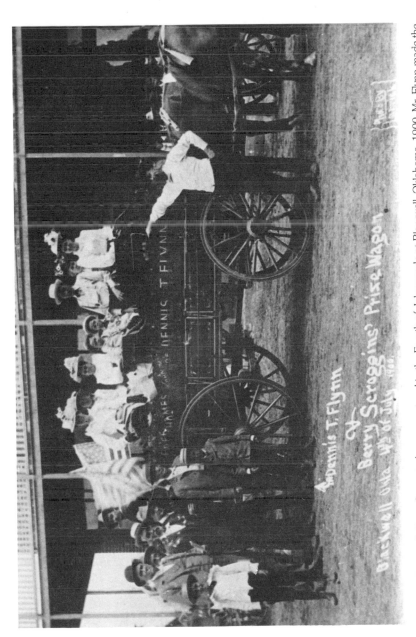

Dennis T. Flynn with Berry Scroggins' wagon, entered in the Fourth of July parade at Blackwell, Oklahoma, 1900. Mr. Flynn made the principal speech during the celebration. Courtesy of the Western History Collections, University of Oklahoma Library.

Chapter 3

EARLY STATEHOOD

With the flourish of a quill pen made from the wing feather of an Oklahoma eagle, Teddy Roosevelt signed the proclamation creating a single state out of the Twin Territories on November 16, 1907. Word was relayed via an open telegraph line to Guthrie, the new capital, where the event was announced by the firing of a six-shooter into the air. The celebration began. A miniature cannon fired a 17-volley salute. Governor Charles N. Haskell, looking strangely out of place in a long black coat, walked to the steps of the Carnegie Library for his swearing-in. A symbolic marriage was held between a cowboy and an Indian maid, marking the union of the white population and one-third of the Indians in the United States who resided in the new state. The saloons, due to close at midnight because of the prohibition clause in the new constitution, did their best to dispose of their stocks of liquor. The pandemonium that characterized the settlement of the Oklahoma frontier seemed distilled in the festivities that marked its closing.

The bitterness of those opposed to the new arrangement—blacks anticipating discriminatory laws, Indians unhappy with their loss of rights, immigrants and others opposed to prohibition—were completely ignored by the newspaper reporters present. Across the country the theme of the reporting stirred the blood of Americans: the last pioneers were celebrating the birth of their state. The American dream was intact. Accounts of the event emphasized the economic promise of Oklahoma and the "progressivism" of its constitution. Great numbers of people pulled up stakes, usually in surrounding states, and headed for the area. Prominent among these in-migrants were many English, Irish, Scottish, and Welsh immigrants.

As a result, over the first two decades of the life of the new state the population of British or Irish birth or parentage expanded im-

26

pressively. The first generation—that is, those born in the Old World—peaked in 1910 and then declined steadily. Sooners with one or both parents born in England and Scotland expanded steadily in numbers over the entire period. Inhabitants of Welsh or Irish parentage became more numerous during the decade after 1910, but declined over the 1920s. Overall, from World War I to the federal census of 1930, the total of first- and second-generation British and Irish within the state hovered around an all-time high of 30,000.

Between 1907 and 1930 newcomers to Oklahoma from Great Britain and Ireland shared characteristics that distinguished them from the American-born population of the state and from their countrymen in other areas of the United States. As in earlier decades they remained generally older than their Oklahoma neighbors. Men were in the majority over women by a ratio of about 3 to 2. The newcomers were more likely than countrymen in other sections of the United States to have married outside of their national group. About 85 percent of married males and 79 percent of married females had native-born spouses. All four national groups displayed an obvious trend towards less time in the New World with each passing decade, but by 1930 about half of all British- and Irish-born inhabitants had been in the United States over fifteen years. Men were more likely than women to have been in the country over twenty years. The occupational patterns of British and Irish in Oklahoma differed markedly from their countrymen in other parts of the United States. In Oklahoma there was a far greater likelihood that members of these groups would be engaged in agricultural pursuits. In urban areas of the state, the great majority of British and Irish were in the skilled ranks and higher. The significant proportion of individuals in unskilled ranks visible in the East Coast cities, particularly among the Irish, was absent.

Over the same period the distribution of British and Irish immigrants in Oklahoma changed. As shown in Figure 2, the English and Irish population in 1910 were spread over the entire state. Increasingly, however, newcomers from these two groups and their children were departing rural areas bound for the cities. The Irish led this transition; by 1920 the majority of immigrants from the Green Isle resided in the city. British-born groups followed so rapidly that by 1930 the Scots, English, and Welsh were predominantly urban. The trek towards Oklahoma's cities was even more pronounced among the second generation; the children of all four groups were far less likely than their parents to reside in rural areas. Oklahoma

City was the most popular urban center for British and Irish on the 1910 and 1920 censuses. On the 1930 enumeration Tulsa had a larger population of Scottish, Welsh, and Irish newcomers than its southern neighbor. But the majority of English-born still favored Oklahoma City.

It was clear that statehood was imminent shortly before the annual convention of the Twin Territorial Federation of Labor in Shawnee in 1906. Fortunately for labor organizers, the Four Brotherhoods of the railroad and the Farmers' Union were also meeting in the city. A joint board of ten members was formed by the convened groups and charged with outlining a labor program for the upcoming constitutional convention. As a result, articles sympathetic to labor were written into the Constitution. They allowed workers to sue for compensation in the case of job injury. The workday in public works and underground in the mines was limited to eight hours. The employment of children was prohibited in hazardous jobs and the use of convict labor was severely restricted. A department of labor and an office of chief mine inspector were created, both under the direction of individuals elected by the people. These achievements, significant in a state where most delegates were agriculturally oriented and unaware of any "industrialization" in the territories, resulted from the labors of British and Irish mine union officials.

The exact details of the interests that united the Farmers' Union and the industrial workers of Oklahoma at the constitutional convention are unclear. Doubtless farmers believed that high wages for industrial workers would allow the purchase of more farm products. Both groups shared the same enemies, notably the electric and power companies and the railroad. But more than anything else, the alliance could be credited to the political clout of the unions who represented a significant number of alert voters and the skills of immigrant mine union leaders. A three-man labor legislative committee lobbied so effectively that 75 percent of the members of the convention were pledged in advance to vote for labor programs. Peter Hanraty, finished third in the voting for president of the convention. Later, as vice-president, he shared power with president William "Alfalfa Bill" Murray of Tishomingo who represented the agricultural forces. It was organized labor's finest hour in Oklahoma.

Hanraty was one of two foreign-born delegates at the constitutional convention; the other was Joseph J. Curl. Born in Bristol, England, Curl came to Ohio as a child. In 1903 he arrived in Bartlesville where he became a very successful oil developer, banker and

Kate Barnard, Oklahoma's first Commissioner of Charities and Corrections. Courtesy of the Oklahoma Historical Society.

builder of street railroads. Elected as a Democrat to represent the Fifty-seventh District at the convention. He performed his mission quietly and efficiently.

The most striking person of British and Irish extraction in attendance at the convention, not as a delegate but as an observer, was Kate Barnard. Born in Nebraska of Irish parents, Kate Barnard was an active reformer in the cause of children's rights, prison reform, and women's suffrage at the time of the convention. Her close friend, Peter Hanraty, was instrumental in designing the Office of Commissioner of Charities and Corrections, perhaps specifically for Miss Barnard. Denied the vote because of her sex, she ran for office and was the most popular candidate in the state, out-polled the governor, and plunged into the job with fervor. Among her most notable achievements were the rescue of Oklahoma prisoners from the terrible cruelty of Kansas prison mines, her successful efforts to build an Oklahoma state prison where prisoners were treated humanely, and the recovery of $2 million budgeted for use by Indian orphans and misappropriated by crooked politicians.

She was devoutly religious and made effective use of religious themes in her appeals to the citizens of Oklahoma. Addressing the legislators of Oklahoma after her discovery of juvenile prisoners from Oklahoma slaving under terrible conditions as contract convicts in the Lansing prison mines of Kansas, she reminded them to "think of the Saviour that took little children into his arms and blessed them." What would we say, she demanded, if He were to return and ask us, "What are my little ones doing here?" She stirred the conscience of fundamentalist Protestants most of whom were unaware of her Catholicism. Successfully re-elected, she served a second term before retiring from public life. When she died on February 23, 1930, her last will and testament prayed that "the youth of the world may emulate me in dedicating their own lives to securing justice for the poor of their generation as I did for mine." Her prayer went unheeded.

Between statehood and the Great Depression, coal mining in Oklahoma achieved its greatest success and its most dismal failure. In the years immediately before statehood the number of large mines grew impressively and it was feared that smaller operators would disappear. Around 1910, however, the number of small mines began to increase rapidly. This was caused by the presence of a surplus of skilled miners, who went to work on the many coal seams lying near the surface. The ready market for such coal among residents of

smaller towns supplied by these small "wagon mines" had b
ignored by the large companies. There was at the same time
impressive increase in the number of "cooperative" mines, run by
groups of workers with little capital on leased land, or sometimes
illegally on land belonging to the larger operators. These mines were
simply attempts by miners to earn a living in the face of a large surplus
of labor.

Miners did not generally share in the prosperity of the industry:
labor problems were becoming increasingly severe. Year after year
as a greater amount of coal was produced, the number of days
worked by a miner during the year declined steadily. By 1914, the
typical miner worked only half time, apparently because of the increasing mechanization of the mines and a decrease in demand for
coal throughout the nation as it was replaced by fuel oil and natural
gas. The owners also blamed high wages, but coal which cost a little
over $2 per ton to produce was selling for over $8 per ton in towns a
short distance from the mines. Indeed, by limiting production in an
effort to keep prices high, the owners caused many to turn to fuel
oil for heating. World War I temporarily solved these problems. From
1917 to 1920 there was a shortage of miners to meet the strong demand for coal. Although workers did well during the years of wartime
demand, wages never increased as rapidly as profits. In a relatively
short period, most operators made substantially more money than
was necessary to pay off their investment. It was the lull before the
storm.

Beginning in 1922, the coal industry fell on hard times. There
were two phases to this decline: between 1922 and 1929, when
medium-sized mines disappeared; and from 1929 until 1934, when
the large operators deserted the business. The problems of substitu-
tion of oil and gas for coal which had hurt the industry in pre-World
War I days were intensified by a declining market during the Great
Depression. Operators were plagued also with labor problems, beginning with the strike of 1924 to 1927. This strike broke the power
of the United Mine Workers, and all miners were forced to accept a
pay cut. The owners won by using armed mine guards and militia
to protect strikebreakers, usually "hoosiers" — poor rural whites living
in desperate straits throughout the state. Unlike Mexican strikebreakers, who eventually turned to unionism, these "hoosiers" showed
little interest in unions.

Peter Hanraty also had abandoned union organizing and no one
appeared to fill his shoes. After playing a leading role in the con-

stitutional convention, he was elected chief mine inspector, a post he held with distinction. Shortly thereafter he opened a small mine at Panama, Oklahoma, where he had the misfortune of losing both legs in an accident. In the face of demands by union members working at his mine in 1925, Hanraty came out against one of his favorite earlier labor goals, the "closed shop." The mine at Panama was destroyed by a flood in 1927, and he made another brief and unsuccessful attempt at mine ownership near Poteau. He was reduced to working as a state capitol guide until 1930 when his old friend Governor William Murray appointed him a special investigator to the chief mine inspector in the McAlester area. This was the last of a long line of occupations held by this brilliant and practical organizer.

Most important in the decline of the union was dissension among a leadership almost exclusively British and Irish. The earlier labor struggle between Socialists led by Alex Howat and Fred Holt and the pure unionists led by John Wilkinson, Andrew McGary, and William Dalrymple grew very intense by 1914. But the general defeat of the Socialists in the union elections of 1916 reduced them to a very vocal minority in the mining towns. The non-socialists now turned to warring among themselves. Throughout the coal counties, the union divided into factions and the strike of the mid-twenties caught them in this condition. The subsequent defeat of the union further discredited the leadership so that by the time of the Great Depression Oklahoma mining unions were virtually leaderless.

As early as the 1840s travelers had commented on the fine green oil floating on the water in numerous water springs and rivers throughout Indian Territory. Although some oil wells were sunk as early as 1888, they were quickly abandoned. Not until Frank Galbreath discovered high-quality oil at Glenn Pool in 1905 did Oklahoma's oil industry become firmly established. The epidemic of oil strikes which followed attracted an invading army of oilmen from Pennsylvania, West Virginia, Ohio, and Virginia. Among the "wildcatters" who built fortunes in the industry were many of British and Irish extraction.

William Grove Skelly was a man determined to live life to the fullest and he succeeded. The fourth of a family of six children, his father was from Belfast, Ireland, his mother from England. After returning from the Civil War, William Skelly, Sr. settled outside of Erie, Pennsylvania, and went to work as a teamster for an oil company. One by one, as they became big enough, his sons joined him. Thus the young William G. Skelly got his start in the oil business. William Jr. entered the oil fields in his teens, and apart from one brief interruption to serve in the Spanish-American War, spent his life in the oil industry. For twenty years he roamed the American oil world, from Indiana to Illinois to Texas, before becoming the largest operator in Kansas. In 1919 he moved the headquarters of his company to Tulsa. For a man of his business interests he spent an impressive amount of time on civic duties. He served as president of the Tulsa Chamber of Commerce, as a Republican national committeeman from Oklahoma, and as president of the International Petroleum Exposition. His contemporaries commented on his physical prowess and his "Irish love of battle . . . his Irish wit and good nature." At home with any group, from oil field roughnecks to Wall Street bankers, he genuinely liked people.

Bill Skelly was only one, albeit the most important, of the many early oilmen from a second-generation British or Irish background. Among the others, most of whom came to Oklahoma via Pennsylvania, were Patrick and Thomas White, David F. Connelly, Daniel and Martin Moran, Harry McGraw, William J. Sherry, Charles L. McMahon, and Edward I. Hanlon. Typical of all of the others, although his career was more successful than most, was William L. Connelly. Born in Cleveland, Ohio, of Irish parents, Connelly began his career as a roustabout in the oil fields of Bradford, Pennsylvania, in the late 1880s. Over the next sixty years he held practically every job in the oil business, eventually becoming chairman of the board of Sinclair Oil and Gas Company.

One of the many curious sights that accompanied the oil boom in Oklahoma was the expression of nostalgia for Ireland which developed in naming the town of Shamrock in Creek County. In 1913 it was a small country village with two stores and a population of thirty-five people. With the development of the nearby Cushing oil field two years later, the townsite shifted and almost overnight grew to over 10,000 people. Why Shamrock became "Irish" when it was platted because of the expansion was a mystery. It may have had something to do with the Irish background of one of its major real estate developers, Edwin L. Dunn of Tulsa. Green became the town's favorite color: many of its buildings were painted green, the postmaster tinted stamps green. The main street was Tipperary Road, other thoroughfares were called after Cork, Dublin, Ireland, Saint Patrick, and Killarney. One of the town's treasures was a "Blarney Stone," sold to the residents by an enterprising salesman. The *Brogue* and the *Blarney* were the town's two newspapers. Shamrock was as tough as other oil boom towns, with more than its share of saloons and gambling halls. "Pretty Boy" Floyd robbed a bank there in 1932, the last major event in the town's history. Shamrock was in sharp decline, and the bank robbery was the final blow. Today, Tipperary Road is deserted and about 200 people live along the wide sidewalks and boulevards that testify to the town's former glory.

Oklahomans had a difficult time accepting the religion of some of the newcomers. The decade of World War I was a particularly rocky time for the Catholic church and for Irish Catholics. Differences of opinion between Catholics and native Protestants over prohibiting alcoholic beverages came to a head in the "sacramental wine case." The "Bone Dry Law" passed by the Oklahoma legislature in 1917 forbade both the importation and possession of alcoholic beverages including sacramental wine, thereby making the celebration of mass illegal. Some supporters of the prohibition law seemed genuinely concerned that religious exclusions would gut a prohibition law. But the prime force sustaining the new law was anti-Catholic bigotry which remained strong in the state until World War II.

A religious exclusion to the "Bone Dry Law" was eventually won in court, but anti-Catholic sentiment touched the lives of immigrants and their children. The defensiveness of Catholics spurred intense efforts to display their patriotism. At the urging of the clergy during World War I, Catholic children, including many from families headed by Irish and British fathers, joined the Oklahoma School Children's Patriotic League with its motto "My Country, may she ever be right, but right or wrong, my country." The patriotism and sacrifice of Catholics in World War I had little impact on many natives: after the war anti-Catholic sentiment grew more intense. Anti-Catholic newspapers were widely circulated in Oklahoma, and anti-Catholic lecturers were popular. Catholics were denied many jobs. And the Oklahoma Americanization Society attempted to get a referendum approved by voters to require that all children attend public schools.

The most severe threat to the Catholic church and to British and Irish Catholics was posed by the Ku Klux Klan. Part of a nationwide organization in the 1920s whose activities were initially directed against lawbreakers, the Oklahoma Klan quickly turned against Catholics and Jews. In the City of Tulsa, Klan activities against Catholics were very strong. In 1923 Catholic schoolteachers in the city were fired as the result of systematic efforts by the KKK. Other city agencies and contractors were pressured to fire Catholics. The engineer in charge of the construction of the Spavinaw Water Project in Tulsa was given a list of his Catholic employees and told to fire them by

Patrick J. Blessing

Shamrock, Oklahoma, at the height of its prosperity in 1914. Courtesy of Mrs. R. M. Wyatt and of the Western History Collections, University of Oklahoma Library.

the KKK. When he refused, the mayor and some city council members called him in and unsuccessfully attempted to get him to comply with the discriminatory order. The Klan obviously had widespread support in important places.

In response to this activity, Irish-American Catholic oilmen in Tulsa hired an individual to attend Ku Klux Klan meetings and list the membership. The list was then circulated among influential Tulsa Catholics with a recommendation that they refuse to do business with Klan members. The Catholic church itself went on a statewide offensive in a low-key manner. Catholics were advised by their priests to remember the danger posed by the hooded empire when they voted in elections. When the *Daily Oklahoman* criticized this "political activity" by the Church, Irish-American Father J. F. McGuire answered the charge in a front-page letter to the newspaper. Ironically, Ku Klux Klan efforts to get Catholics out of politics had the opposite effect.

But there was support for Catholics in some areas of society. Most of the anti–Ku Klux Klan activity was conducted by the more educated "people of intelligence and culture." Irish-American Catholic Mathew J. Kane continued to serve on the Oklahoma Supreme Court. Even among those "decent citizens" on the bottom of the social scale in many small towns scattered throughout the state, non-Catholics stood their ground against the rising tide of fanaticism. In her classic, *Prairie City,* Angie Debo tells a story that was typical of events in many small towns. At considerable cost to himself, a Protestant ex-army sergeant, Kenneth Martin, carried on a one-man war in his town against the Klan's attacks on an Irish neighbor, Bill O'Hagan, who had served under him in World War I. These broadminded citizens eventually won out over the Klan. Despite a mild flare-up of anti-Catholicism when Al Smith ran for President in 1928, after the fall of the KKK in the mid-twenties relations between Catholic and Protestant Oklahomans improved steadily.

British Protestants became well established within the state during the early years of statehood. The most highly placed Protestant immigrant churchman was Scottish-born Methodist Bishop Robert McIntyre, who came to the United States as a young man and graduated from Vanderbilt University. After serving as pastor in a number of churches in Illinois, Colorado, and California, Reverend McIntyre retired from active ministry upon his election as bishop of Oklahoma. He served from 1908 to 1914 and was an accomplished preacher and administrator, in addition to authoring a popular book of poetry. Like many British churchmen of his day, Bishop McIntyre enriched religious life within Oklahoma by adding an intellectual depth to the state's basically rural Protestant churches.

Like their countrymen in other sections of the United States, Oklahoma's Irish made their mark in politics and the law. Among the most notable was Patrick J. Hurley. One of eight children of Irish immigrant parents, Hurley's father, Pierce, had arrived in the United States in 1868. Young Pat was born in Texas where his father drifted from job to job, farming and punching cattle, before he moved to Indian Territory in 1882. The boy's first job, at the age of eleven, was as a miner for the Atoka Coal and Mining Company. Largely self-educated, Pat eventually worked his way through law school and became attorney for the Choctaw tribe. Following decorated service in World War I, he returned to private practice in Tulsa. His quiet and successful political work for the Republican party and his backing of Herbert Hoover, whom he first met in Belgium after World War I, resulted in an appointment as assistant secretary of war in 1929. It was the first step in a long and distinguished career in public service which was to stretch across the globe.

When the Oklahoma Criminal Court of Appeals was created in 1908, Thomas Henchion Doyle was appointed an associate justice. He was successfully re-elected five times, and for eight years, 1915 to 1923, served as chief presiding justice. Doyle, the son of Irish immigrants, was born in 1862 in Massachusetts. He moved to Kansas as a boy, where, after working on the railroad, he read law under a small town lawyer in Ottawa. Moving to Perry, Oklahoma, at the time of the settlement, he began practice as a lawyer. Twice elected to the Territorial Legislative Assembly he became a leading spokesman for single statehood. After completion of his fifth term on the court, he retired from public life in 1944. He was widely respected for his legal mind. Of him a colleague wrote: "Judge Doyle made the law his chief shrine in worthy spheres, yet he gave to all the forces of the social order his deepest interest and able service."

Also impressive on the Oklahoma bench was Matthew J. Kane, born in 1863 in New York of Irish immigrant parents. After graduating from Georgetown University, he moved to Kansas where he practiced law for two years prior to moving to Kingfisher in 1889. He was a member of the constitutional convention, and in the first election after statehood was elected to the state supreme court. In his third term on the court, he was elected chief justice, and served until his death in 1924.

The City of Tulsa produced a number of prominent Irish-American politicians and lawyers over the decades between statehood and the Great Depression. Charles O'Connor was born in Missouri in 1878, the son of immigrant parents from County Kerry. He became a lawyer in Boulder, Colorado, in 1904, where he practiced until he left for Tulsa in 1919. As Republican candidate for Oklahoma's First District, he won election to congress in 1928 and served for one term. Timothy Leahy, whose father was from Tipperary and mother from Limerick, was born in Kansas in 1868. After graduation from law school he came to Tulsa where he immediately became involved in politics as a Democrat. He was a member of the constitutional convention in 1906. After a distinguished career in private practice he was appointed special assistant United States attorney general in 1927 to prosecute Osage Indian murder cases.

Other Irish-Americans were directly involved in city government in Tulsa. Michael J. McNulty, born in Dublin in 1887, served Tulsa successively as city treasurer, city commissioner, and mayor pro tem, before establishing 225-bed Morningside Hospital, one of the finest hospitals in the United States. As Tulsa's prosecuting attorney, Pat Malloy, born of Irish parents in Salix, Iowa, in 1885, became the only prosecutor in Oklahoma history ever to lose a case because he was too persuasive a speaker. A convicted defendant in a successful appeal claimed Malloy was such a smooth talker that the jurors fell under a spell and were oblivious to the facts of the alleged crime. After two terms in office he resigned and embarked on a very successful career as an oil producer. Attorney Thomas J. Lyons, a second-generation Irishman, was very active behind the scenes in city politics and served on Governor Walton's supreme court commission. Thomas J. Quinn, born in St. Louis of Irish immigrant parents, served on the school board and as commissioner of police and fire. In addition to membership in the Democratic party, McNulty, Malloy, Lyons, and Quinn were all devout Catholics and active members of the Knights of Columbus. The importance of their religious and social affiliation in spurring the successful vendetta waged against them by Protestant Republicans over the years 1914–16 remains a mystery, but it does appear more than mere coincidence.

The Great Depression signaled the end of an era for the British and Irish in Oklahoma. The transition was marked by the deaths of a number of prominent people. Bitter and disillusioned, Kate Barnard died alone in 1930. Three years later, a discouraged Peter Hanraty died of a heart attack, caused, many believe, by an overdose of alcohol. However, the 1930 death of Mother Jones in Maryland at over 100 years of age, had the most profound impact on British and Irish workingmen, particularly miners. News of her death spread rapidly throughout the coalfields of Oklahoma. A eulogy, "The Death of Mother Jones," became the region's most popular song, partly because of the plaintive singing of a young railroad telegrapher, Gene Autry. But the words of the song emphasizing courage and resistance in the face of suffering and deprivation had obvious appeal to miners trying to cope with the ravages of the Depression in a rapidly declining industry. The unity displayed at Mother Jones' passing was the last hurrah for immigrant labor in the state. The heroic age of the British and Irish in Oklahoma had ended.

Chapter 4
GREAT DEPRESSION AND WORLD WAR II

When William H. "Alfalfa Bill" Murray returned to Oklahoma from a five-year self-imposed exile in Bolivia in August 1929, the state was in terrible economic condition. He immediately convened a meeting of the "survivors" of the constitutional convention who agreed that government in Oklahoma had failed. A return to old values was essential. In short, Murray should run for governor. Alfalfa Bill's subsequent stunning election victory in 1930 confirmed the judgment of his old friends: in the midst of acute economic and social disruption Oklahomans looked desperately to the past for guidance. And the past is what they got from Murray. His public pronouncements on politicians, universities, society women, blacks (he called them "niggers"), the organized poor, and innumerable other topics put him at least a generation behind mainstream America. Newspaper columnists and cartoonists were delighted. By 1932, apart from Franklin D. Roosevelt, Murray was the best-known governor in the country. To some Americans he had appeal, but to most he was a symbol of all that was wrong with rural America. The frontier dream had faded. The sturdy pioneer had been reduced to the level of the Joads, drifting west along Highway 66, dreaming the golden dream despite the shame of their poverty.

As governor, Murray did little more than was necessary to ensure the bare survival of the state. He even opposed New Deal legislation that eventually initiated the recovery of Oklahoma. Thus the state's attractiveness as a destination for immigrants was greatly reduced, and there was a 40 percent decline in the population of British and Irish birth and parentage. At the same time, the move towards urban residence by these newcomers, under way since statehood, continued unabated. By 1940 only 17 percent of both groups still lived on farms. The great majority of British and Irish naturalized in Oklahoma's federal courts during the 1930s were over forty years of age and had resided in the United States for over twenty-one years. Three out of four Depression petitioners for naturalization in the Muskogee district federal court had an incredible twenty-six years or more in the New World. Over all, fewer immigrants in the younger age brackets petitioned for naturalization in Oklahoma during the 1930s than in any other decade. But there was no significant movement by British and Irish out of the state with the Okie migration to California. Most immigrant farmers were more prosperous than the element of rural society that furnished the great majority of California-bound migrants. The decline in numbers of British and Irish in Oklahoma during the Great Depression was the result of reduced in-migration coupled with the deaths of older immigrants.

The wartime decade of the forties was marked by the movement of hundreds of thousands of young people out of Oklahoma's rural areas. Some went to cities within the state, where by the end of the decade most Oklahomans lived. But the majority left the state for the military or for defense work in other states, particularly Texas and California, never to return. The economic recovery which began under the New Deal was intensified by mobilization for World War II. The state did well as a result of the war. In terms of federal contracts and facilities Oklahoma ranked eighteenth among all states, and Tulsa and Oklahoma City were in the top ten cities in the country in terms of expanding job rates. Initially as governor, later as United States senator, Robert Kerr built on this base to bring Oklahoma into the twentieth-century industrial world. As a result of his efforts, in 1948 the state's industrial development grew almost four times as fast as that of the nation as a whole.

The economic development of Oklahoma during the forties provided jobs which attracted British and Irish immigrants thereby arresting the steady decline in their numbers within the state which began with the Great Depression. But the level of in-migration of English, Scottish, Irish, and Welsh newcomers is far higher than suggested by the census figures, which held steady at about 2,500 in 1940 and 1950. These over all figures obscure the replacement with new arrivals of a great many older immigrants who died. The level of in-migration of individuals of British or Irish parentage was never high enough to offset losses of second-generation Oklahomans through out-migration and death. As a result the numbers of Sooners of British or Irish parentage declined steadily over the period.

As in earlier decades most males from England, Ireland, Scotland, and Wales arriving in Oklahoma during the wartime decade were at least forty years old and had a significant amount of time in the United States. The majority who petitioned for naturalization during the forties were over forty years of age and had been in the New World over twenty years. Moreover, as in earlier days, an impressive proportion of Oklahoma's British and Irish held white-collar jobs, generally on the managerial levels in the new defense industries. For the first time since the prosperous years in the coal industry around World War I, the 1940s witnessed the arrival of many blue-collar immigrants, usually enlisted men in the armed forces stationed at military camps in the state. What proportion of these individuals remained in Oklahoma after military service is unknown; clearly some did. Finally, the proportion of immigrants in urban areas continued to increase steadily, not only in Oklahoma City and Tulsa but in many of the smaller urban places throughout the state that had succeeded in attracting defense plants.

The majority of newcomers from Britain and Ireland arriving in Oklahoma during the forties were young women who married American servicemen in the British Isles and came to the States with their husbands. Most "war-brides" — as they were commonly called — were English. Next in importance were Scots and Welsh. The few Irish were generally from the north of Ireland. Despite the label "war bride," many of them had married after the war. Indeed, up through the fifties there was a steady stream of immigrant military brides to the Sooner State. As a result, since World War II the great majority of British women naturalized in Oklahoma have been under thirty years old and in the country for less than fifteen years. How many women arrived in this manner during the forties was unclear but the number hovered around the 500 mark. From 1945 until recently there have been over twice as many Englishwomen as Englishmen in Oklahoma.

Military brides had an experience different from that of British and Irish newcomers to the Sooner State before World War II: they came directly to the area and thus were spared the long years of adjustment which earlier arrivals had spent in other parts of the United States. As a result they experienced a deeper shock upon arrival and an adjustment at times more difficult. Most war-brides comment on the impact of arrival on Oklahomans and upon themselves. The natives were surprised to discover that war-brides talked and looked little different from Sooners. Much of this reaction was the result of a general lack of information on Europe, especially in rural areas. War-brides who have lived in Oklahoma since World War II comment on how much more cosmopolitan the people are today. For the immigrant brides, the weather and the people took some adjustment. Arriving in Oklahoma City on a humid 103-degree day in the summer of 1946, one war-bride thought that she had arrived in a "suburb of hell." But there was no significant movement back to England. Over time an adjustment was made: about half of all war-brides were naturalized before they had five years in the United States. As one woman put it, "eventually the people became as friendly as they seemed on the surface." And air-conditioning solved the problems of summer heat, although many still talk nostalgically of English summers. Doubtless in part because of the uniqueness of their manner of arrival, war-brides have provided the backbone of the membership of British clubs in Oklahoma since World War II.

The appointment of Irish-Canadian Bishop Francis C. Kelley to the Diocese of Oklahoma in 1924 signaled the beginning of the arrival to power of clergy initially of Irish background, later of Irish birth. Born on Prince Edward Island, Kelley was one of the most influential churchmen in the United States at the time of his appointment to Oklahoma. He was a nationally known figure for his work with the Catholic Church Extension Society on behalf of missionary parishes throughout the United States. Also well known for his diplomatic efforts because of his work in settling problems between the Vatican and the Italian government at the end of World War I, he vigorously opposed the anti-clerical Mexican Revolution. As a scholar, diplomat, and evangelist, he seemed a perfect choice to head the Catholic Church in the Sooner State.

Until he passed away in 1946 Kelley did a commendable job of lowering barriers between Catholics and non-Catholics in Oklahoma — no small achievement considering the record of the early twenties. Shortly after his appointment he began an extensive campaign to visit all parts of the state, making a special effort to talk to non-Catholics. In a missionary effort which he launched to counteract anti-Catholic propaganda, his use of the radio made history and laid the basis for national religious programs in later years. Bishop Kelley's work was accompanied by a decline in anti-Catholic activity, but such outbursts were far from unknown. A large well attended anti-Catholic meeting was held in Tulsa in the early 1930s, and Catholics found it very difficult to gain employment in the city's public schools. Eugene Maple, manager of the state's insurance fund, claimed in 1935 that Ed Benson, chairman of the Oklahoma Industrial Commission, fired him for refusing to dismiss all Catholics as Benson had ordered. On

August 15, 1940, armed with a search warrant, the Federal Bureau of Investigation conducted a search for arms in the rectory of Saint Joseph's Church in Oklahoma City. The incident, never satisfactorily explained, marked the end of overt discrimination against the Roman Church in Oklahoma.

Beginning with his arrival in Oklahoma, Bishop Kelley made a special effort to recruit native-born priests for a diocese where Belgian and Dutch priests were the dominant group. By 1940 he had succeeded in increasing the numbers of diocesan priests by about one-third, which included many native sons. But the needs of the diocese went beyond the numbers of native-born entering the priesthood, and Kelley encouraged some Canadian-Irish priests to move to Oklahoma. Among these were Gavin Monaghan, James Rooney, and A. O. Murphy. Three English-born priests arrived in Oklahoma during the thirties, Reginald Wright, Bernard Loftus and Eric Beevers, together with an Irish-Englishman, Joseph Duffey. Bishop Kelley also persuaded a community of nuns from Ireland, the Holy Ghost Sisters, to come to Tulsa to staff a school for black children. One Irish priest who arrived uninvited at this time, James McNamee, tested the toleration of Bishop Kelley and two of his successors.

James McNamee was born April 18, 1902, in Longford, Ireland. At the suggestion of an uncle who served as a priest in Missouri, young McNamee decided to attend Kenrick Seminary in St. Louis, Missouri. Upon ordination in 1925 he became a priest at Holy Family Cathedral in Tulsa, the first of a number of appointments to parishes in Okmulgee, Edmond, and the Oil Capital. McNamee's beliefs on Catholic procedures and practices were at least a generation ahead of his time. He first came to public attention in 1937 when his suggestion that the language of the mass be changed from Latin to English sparked a national controversy. Knowledgeable Oklahoma Catholics agreed that such a change would greatly improve the image of the church by demonstrating that it was not an alien religion as many fundamentalist Protestants believed. Father McNamee spent World War II as a chaplain with the United States Army, returning to Oklahoma at the conclusion of hostilities as concerned as ever with reform of religious and social life.

Bishop Kelley was succeeded in office by a man whose background was somewhat similar to his own. Eugene J. McGuinness was born of Irish parents in Pennsylvania. Shortly after ordination he went to work with Kelley's Catholic Church Extension Society. His eighteen years with the organization were spent aiding Catholics in poorer regions of rural America. For seven years before his arrival in Oklahoma in 1945, McGuinness served as bishop of Raleigh, North Carolina. Upon arrival in the Diocese of Oklahoma, he set out immediately to recruit priests wherever they could be found. This effort took him to the major supplier of priests in the world at the time, Ireland. Among the Irishmen who came to Oklahoma as a result are many who still serve in parishes in the state including Gerald O'Nolan, Philip Donohoe, Dennis G. Hanrahan, Mike J. Hanrahan, Mike Hughes, John G. O'Brien, Michael Keating and Fintan McMahon. There was also a considerable influx of Irish-American priests at this time, many of them from Bishop McGuinness' state of birth, Pennsylvania. It was the beginning of a period where there was a very obvious Irish presence in the Oklahoma Catholic church.

The most famous Oklahoma politician of British or Irish background over the last several decades was Patrick J. Hurley, who became secretary of war in December 1929. Committed to his friend Herbert Hoover, he was vehement in defense of the President in the 1932 presidential campaign. Although an outspoken foe of New Deal legislation, he was vitally interested in solving the problems of industrial society, and his 1932 suggestion that the workday be reduced was well received even by labor. Hurley eventually went to work in defense of the National Recovery Act, "Marquis of Queensbury rules for business," he called it, much to the displeasure of his old friend Hoover. His legal efforts during the thirties to obtain redress for American oil companies whose property was expropriated by the Mexican government brought him to the attention of President Franklin D. Roosevelt, who recommended him for a military appointment at the outbreak of World War II. As personal representative of the Army Chief of Staff in 1941 he was an able administrator, organizer, and diplomat who succeeded in getting supplies through a Japanese blockade to the beleaguered defenders of the Philippines. This was the first of a number of tough diplomatic assignments which he held during World War II, serving with distinction in New Zealand, the Middle East, Russia, and China. Shortly after the war he returned to private practice in Tulsa.

Pat Hurley never forgot his boyhood in Coalgate, and was as proud of Oklahoma as it was of him. His life was the frontier dream writ large. He had gone out and conquered other worlds, constantly seeking new challenges. The sense of wonder at his own achievements which he occasionally expressed, understandable in an ex-breaker boy from the coal mines of Indian Territory, drew sarcasm

Patrick J. Hurley greeting Mao Tse-Tung, Yenan, China, November 7, 1944. Courtesy of the Western History Collections, University of Oklahoma Library.

from some with more favored backgrounds. Hurley was no elitist. Indeed, one of his great strengths was his talent for treating people equally despite social status, skin color, nationality, or religion. American Indians, who claimed him as one of their own, black victims of Tulsa's bloody race riot of 1921, Mexicans, Saudi Arabians, Iranians, Russians, and Chinese were all impressed with the dignity and respect he accorded them. His loyalties were proverbial, but never blind, and impressed two presidents. His failings were those of one who cared too much for the American system that had made him what he was. His deep respect for American freedom, justice, civil liberty, education, and self-government—unfashionable even in his day led him to speak out against colonialism and communism because they denied these gifts to their citizens. He was decent, courageous, and honest in an age in which there was much temptation for men to forget the value of these virtues in themselves.

Also important in Oklahoma politics during this period was Olney Foster Flynn, the son of the famous Irish-American Republican delegate to Congress from Oklahoma Territory, Dennis Flynn. After attending Harvard University and serving in the United States Navy during World War I, Olney Flynn began his working life as a teller in an Oklahoma City bank. In 1927 he formed the Flynn Oil Company and shortly thereafter became a director of the Santa Fe Railroad. From 1944 to 1946 he served as mayor of Tulsa and is credited with introducing sound fiscal management procedures to that city. The Republican party nominated Flynn for the governor's race in the first postwar election in 1946. He lost the election by a slim margin to Democrat Roy J. Turner and returned to private business life.

By 1950, the Oklahoma of "Alfalfa Bill" Murray was rapidly disappearing. Much of it had left with the stream of migrants out of the state's rural areas, beginning as a trickle during World War I and becoming a torrent over the Depression years and later. Although many who departed were replaced by skilled out-of-state industrial workers, including some British and Irish, these more educated newcomers never arrived in numbers sufficient to prevent significant over all loss of population. But perhaps the cruel joke that the Okie migration to California had raised the I.Q. of both states was partly true. Over the same period Oklahomans moved from the farm to the city. By 1950 most inhabitants lived in places of over 2,500 population. While it would be misleading to call many of these places "urban" in any strict sense of the word, in general most Oklahomans were now less isolated than they had been in earlier decades. The process of change during the forties was somewhat intensified by the arrival of war-brides accompanied by Sooners who had visited Europe and other parts of the world as guests of Uncle Sam. Oklahomans were becoming increasingly familiar with the world beyond their state and the Southwest. The past had certainly not been discarded, but the Oklahoma of Bob Kerr's dreams was in the process of being realized.

Chapter 5

SINCE 1950

The turbulence that characterized the first run of 1889 masked a severe problem: the opening of land came too late in the season to allow the planting of crops. It was an omen ignored by settlers. Yet time after time since 1889 this "brand new state" with its unparalleled combination of manpower, minerals, and land has seemed on the verge of realizing its promise. The failure to do so up until the eve of World War II was blamed successively on the boll weevil, agricultural decline, weather, and the Great Depression. But clearly the major problem was that many of Oklahoma's social and economic crises were beyond the ability of rural state politicians. Federal involvement in national economic planning during the late 1930s and 1940s initiated real industrial growth in Oklahoma and rewarded the patience of a great number of impoverished Sooners desperate for a better tomorrow. The federal interest and aid coupled with the vision and competence of a number of governors, the most important of whom was Robert S. Kerr, has brought steady economic growth since World War II. Still the potential remains far from realization: Oklahoma is not yet "fully grown."

The development of industry in the state since 1950 has attracted a fairly steady influx of British and Irish. Over the fifties the numbers of Oklahomans born in England and Wales expanded while the numbers of Scots and Irish declined. But during the sixties, the total number of Irish grew by about 30 percent while the other three groups declined. All together there were a total of only 2,260 British- and Irish-born Oklahomans on the 1970 census, fewer than the total in the old Twin Territories around the turn of the century. Over the past several decades the number of Oklahomans of British and Irish parentage has declined steadily to 9,818. Moreover, the British and Irish population are becoming more urbanized: by 1960 almost half of the entire group lived in Oklahoma City and Tulsa. Reflecting the spread of industry throughout the state since then, only 39 percent were in the two largest cities in the state in 1970. Many British and Irish at that time were located in smaller urban places throughout Oklahoma.

Since 1950 immigrants from England, Ireland, Wales, and Scotland who journeyed to the Sooner State have been younger and more educated than their countrymen of earlier days, although most of them got some of their education after arrival in the United States. Only three out of ten males and one out of ten females married within their own national group. Over 70 percent of British and Irish naturalized during the 1950s and 1960s were under forty years of age. Their occupations reflect their higher education; about four out of five immigrants naturalized since 1950 hold white-collar jobs. Moreover, there was an impressive tendency to apply for naturalization with fewer years in the United States than in early days. Seventy percent naturalizing in the fifties, 80 percent in the sixties, and 60 percent in the seventies had been in the country less than a decade.

There were several principal reasons why British or Irish immigrants came to Oklahoma after 1950. As in earlier years there has been a steady in-migration of military brides, particularly during the fifties. Other newcomers arrived in the state to take a promised job or were transferred here from out of state by national companies. In Tulsa many first- and second-generation immigrants working for American Airlines were transferred there from other states. A third group, all male, were assigned to Oklahoma during military service and stayed or returned to the state at the completion of their enlistment. Oklahoma City had a fair sprinkling of these individuals. Finally many came to the Sooner State because of encouragement from a relative who had migrated in earlier years. Altogether, marriage to an Oklahoman, job opportunities, transfers by national companies, military service, or joining a relative account for the overwhelming majority of British and Irish immigrants who have arrived in Oklahoma over the past quarter century.

As a result of Bishop McGuinness' recruiting efforts in Ireland, by the mid-fifties there were about twenty Irish-born priests in Oklahoma and a clear Irish presence in the Catholic church in the state. The movement brought about a certain amount of chain migration: several priests encouraged to come to Oklahoma by McGuinness had in turn persuaded relatives to join them. It was common for most Irish-born priests to socialize regularly with each other. Some in

Bishop McGuinness at the groundbreaking ceremonies for the Saint Francis Seminary, Oklahoma City. Courtesy of the *Sooner Catholic*.

northern Oklahoma developed social networks which included Irish priests in southern Kansas. The sixties witnessed a steady decline in output and the eventual disappearance of this clerical pipeline from Ireland. Today most Sons of Erin in the priesthood who came at the height of Bishop McGuinness' recruitment campaign are either planning to retire or have retired. It is doubtful that the Irish will ever again become the presence in the Oklahoma Catholic church that they were during the fifties and sixties.

Over the 1950s, Father James McNamee came into his own as the primary Oklahoma Catholic critic of the church bureaucracy and of society. He attempted to persuade the church to divest itself of excess property, pointing out that wealth involved coercive power and was "disastrous to a church committed to teach and sanctify rather than to command and coerce." As pastor of Tulsa's Madaline Parish in 1962, he led the first Catholic parish in the world to join the National Council of Churches. Father McNamee never hesitated to speak out on religious matters despite the frequent clash between his vision of Christianity and the views of most of his colleagues in the church.

Christianity, to McNamee, represented also a commitment to the real world, not a flight from it. He tackled the shortcomings of society very directly. Speaking to an affluent audience, he accused those who favored population control of being primarily concerned with limiting the ability of the poor to have children on the mistaken assumption that the rich were genetically superior to the poor. "Perhaps," he suggested, "excessive greed for material things is a sign of inferiority: a sort of imbecility rather than mental health." On another occasion he criticized Catholic bishops for their stand on capital punishment by asking, "Isn't it ironic that the very bishops who approve capital punishment are in some cases the same bishops who disapprove of killing the unborn?" In church sermons, public lectures, letters to the newspapers and on the picket line, Father McNamee made known his views on civil rights, drug addiction, pacifism, disarmament, the Vietnam War, individual privacy, abortion laws, literacy tests, anti-Semitism and a variety of other topics. Indeed, it is impossible to find a controversial subject on which he remained silent over his half-century career. When he died in 1975, liberal Catholics, Protestants, and Jews gave him an ecumenical send-off worthy of the folk hero he had become. Conservatives avoided the ceremony.

British and Irish immigrants in Oklahoma today are a rather diverse group. The great majority are white collar, mostly on the

The Reverend James McNamee. Courtesy of Dr. John J. McNamee.

managerial levels of the occupational structure. But there is a fair sprinkling of professionals: medical doctors attracted by the impressive financial rewards of practice in America, one Irish college professor, an Irish oil company executive, and a number of English-born radio announcers who make the most of their accent. Particularly impressive is the proportion of English and Irish immigrants who worked their way from blue-collar backgrounds at home to white-collar jobs in the United States.

Born in County Meath, Ireland, in 1910, Pat Brogan came to America at eighteen years of age when a doctor recommended that he seek a climate better than Ireland to recover from a lung disease. Although he arrived on the eve of the Great Depression, Pat liked America. Coming here fulfilled a boyhood dream, but life was not easy. From Los Angeles to New Orleans he traveled frequently as a hobo, not missing many meals but "postponing a lot of them." His jobs included dishwasher and carnival barker. He was selling burial insurance to sharecroppers in northern Louisiana in 1935—the best job he had in the United States up to that date—when he met Oscar Ameringer, famed socialist editor and organizer. They became good friends and Ameringer eventually invited Brogan to come to Oklahoma. In the Sooner State, Brogan worked as an insurance salesman, milk delivery man and cab driver. He was married in 1947, during his first year in night law school at the old Oklahoma City College of Law. After graduation in 1950 he commenced practice in his own law firm. Today he and his son are partners in the firm of Brogan and Brogan in Oklahoma City. His "roots are in Oklahoma."

Brogan's experiences are typical in many ways of a significant proportion of British and Irish immigrants from poor backgrounds at home who moved up the occupational scale in Oklahoma since World War II. Most were in the United States for some time, generally from ten to twenty years, before they discovered the key to occupational mobility. These individuals are optimists. They believe that they can survive in America regardless of obstacles. The departure from home in their cases represented a vote of confidence in the future: life would be better for them because they would make it better. Time after time as they moved from job to job on the trek to Oklahoma their confidence in their ability to survive was reinforced. By the time of their arrival in the Sooner State they were well adjusted to American society. Particularly impressive among the Irish-born were individuals who left the lowest levels of Dublin society in the fifties, disgusted by the lack of job opportunities, the destitution, the sit-down strikes by masses of unemployed men desperate for work. In the United States most had served in the military and through hard work and effort, invariably including some education, had moved into white-collar jobs. They had no intention of returning home.

There are few discernible differences between British and Irish immigrants in Oklahoma either past or present, although an historical net of finer mesh might uncover some. But the adaptation of their children to the society diverged to some degree. For the British, psychologically speaking, there was no second generation. Outside of checking birth, death, or other vital records, it is impossible to learn the parentage of British Oklahomans since they never identify themselves as English, Scots, or Welsh. Most Sooners of Irish parentage however call themselves "Irish." Still, many second-generation Irish have adapted impressively to Oklahoma society, particularly in religion. A fair sprinkling of Protestants in the state today are the offspring of Irish immigrants who struggled to keep their Catholicism.

English, Irish, and Scots clubs in Oklahoma are stronger than ever, curiously in view of the diminishing presence of the groups, or possibly because of it. There are presently nine such organizations in the Sooner State. Although most clubs are formed around the activities of a particular group, there are few rigid requirements for membership. It is possible to find Irish individuals in British clubs; the reverse however is much more unusual. But the "British" have in Tulsa the British Club and the Scottish Club; in Oklahoma City, the Golden Chain, Scottish Club, and Mid-West Cuppa Club. The BIN Club of Oklahoma City includes the unusual combination of British, Irish, and Newfoundlanders. Although most of the members of the Royal Ascots of Oklahoma City are "trans-Atlantic brides," all of the other British clubs have a large proportion of British immigrants who came to the state because of marriage to a Sooner. The All-Ireland Club of Oklahoma City and the Irish-American Club of Tulsa cater to Oklahomans of Irish birth or parentage. Oklahoma City also hosts one of thirty chapters in the United States of the Irish Georgian Society, devoted to saving Georgian architecture in Ireland. The Welsh are the only group without their own club, but they are eagerly accepted into all of the British organizations.

The influence on Oklahoma of citizens born in England, Ireland, Scotland, and Wales and their children far transcends their numbers in the state. It is impossible to imagine the state's Constitution without the leavening influence of Peter Hanraty and his fellow immigrant political and union leaders. Kate Barnard and James McNamee refused to allow Sooners to forget the most deprived in the society. Politics and the bench were dignified by the presence of Patrick J. Hurley, Charles O'Connor, Thomas J. Lyons, Thomas Henchion Doyle, and Matthew J. Kane. As organizers of the state's important oil industry William Grove Skelly and William L. Connelly had few equals. The Catholic church, aided by Irish-Americans, survived the most intense expression of organized bigotry ever seen in the state, the Ku Klux Klan. Add to the impact of these first- and second-generation Oklahomans the contributions of ordinary Sooners of British or Irish ancestry, and the influence is beyond measure. Indeed it is fair to argue that without immigration from Britain and Ireland there would be no Oklahoma.

The British and Irish are no longer a presence in Oklahoma. Although the numbers are declining slowly, the proportion of English, Irish, Scots, and Welsh in the over all population is declining rapidly. Oklahoma is becoming more Oklahoman each year: the 1970 census showed that over three out of five of the state's inhabitants were born here. The future development of the Sooner State will take place without the challenge to accepted ways provided in the past by enterprising British and Irish immigrants. But in the peaceful political resolution of conflicts, in the immigrant contribution to life in the new state, and in the opportunities which Oklahoma provided for immigrants and their descendants lie the secrets of the American experiment.

BIBLIOGRAPHICAL ESSAY

Given the general non-academic audience to which this work is directed footnotes are omitted. This had the additional advantage of allowing as much text as possible, since there were definite space limitations. But for readers curious about the sources of information the following is offered.

The brevity of this book belies the magnitude of the research on which it is based. It is in fact the distillation of information gleaned from collective biographies of all British and Irish listed on the surviving manuscript schedules of the 1890 federal census of Oklahoma Territory, collective biographies of 200 randomly selected family heads listed on the manuscript schedules of the 1900 federal census for Oklahoma Territory; collective biographies of all petitioners born in Britain or Ireland who filed for naturalization in the district federal courts of Oklahoma over the years 1907–78; a survey of British and Irish families described in all available county "mug" books; a review of all published census reports, regular and special, providing information on our groups within the state; and a review of federal and other governmental reports on the coal-mining industry in Indian Territory and in the State of Oklahoma. Some of the results of processing these data are presented in the Tables.

The statement attributed to Brother John Laracy in Chapter 2 can be found in his memoirs which are quoted extensively in Joseph F. Murphy, *Tenacious Monks* (Shawnee, Oklahoma: Benedictine Color Press, 1974). Kate Barnard's speeches, cited in Chapter 3, are from the collection of newspaper clippings on her life in the Oklahoma Historical Society Library. The Patrick Hurley papers are in the University of Oklahoma Western History Collections. Scattered but useful papers by and about Peter Hanraty are held by the Oklahoma Historical Society.

To develop insights into ethnic life in contemporary Oklahoma detailed questionnaires were mailed to 480 immigrants; about 40 percent were completed and returned in sufficient time to allow inclusion of information in the writing. Moreover, many personal interviews were conducted with individual immigrants.

A number of secondary works were used to supplement the information gleaned from primary sources. The most up-to-date overview of the movement and adjustment of each of the groups in our study can be found in the *Harvard Guide to American Ethnic Groups* (Cambridge: Harvard University Press, 1980). Conditions underlying movement out of England, Scotland, and Wales are reviewed in detail in the series of essays in the special issue "The Social Background of American Immigration," in *Perspectives in American History,* VII (1973); for Ireland, see Oliver MacDonagh, "The Irish Famine Emigration to the United States," in *Perspectives in American History,* X (1976). General coverage of all aspects of cross-Atlantic movement and adjustment can be found in Maldwyn A. Jones, *American Immigration* (Chicago, University of Chicago Press, 1960). Basic data to relate economic and population change throughout the United States with Oklahoma population patterns are provided in Everett S. Lee, *et al., Population Redistribution and Economic Growth, United States,* 1870–1950, Vol. 1 (Philadelphia, American Philosophical Society, 1958).

There are several standard works on Oklahoma history, Arrell M. Gibson, *Oklahoma: A History of Five Centuries* (Norman: University of Oklahoma Press, 1965), is as good as any. This should be supplemented by the imaginative narrative of H. Wayne Morgan and Anne Hodges Morgan, *Oklahoma* (New York: Norton, 1977); and the classic Angie Debo, *Oklahoma, Foot-loose and Fancy-free* (Norman: University of Oklahoma Press, 1949). For an understanding of social life in early Oklahoma, Angie Debo, *Tulsa: From Creek Town to Oil* (Norman: University of Oklahoma Press, 1943) and *Prairie City: The Story of an American Community* (New York: Alfred A. Knopf Inc., 1944), are essential. See also Donald E. Green, ed., *Rural Oklahoma* (Oklahoma City: Oklahoma Historical Society, 1977).

Surprisingly little has been done to study the oil industry and its leading men, but Carl Coke Rister, *Oil, Titan of the Southwest* (Norman: University of Oklahoma Press, 1949), should be perused. No study of the economic transformation of the state over the past three decades is complete without reference to Anne Hodges Morgan, *Robert S. Kerr: The Senate Years* (Norman: University of Oklahoma Press, 1977). For immigrant life in the coal industry see the annual

Patrick J. Blessing

reports of the mine inspector for Indian Territory published by the Government Printing Office, Washington, over the years 1892–1907. See also *Report of the United States Coal Commission* (Washington: Government Printing Office, 1925); Frederick Lynne Ryan, *The Rehabilitation of Oklahoma Coal Mining Communities* (Norman: University of Oklahoma Press, 1935); and *A History of Labor Legislation in Oklahoma* (Norman: University of Oklahoma Press, 1932).

No study has so far been completed of immigrants in radical politics in the State of Oklahoma, rather astounding considering their degree of involvement. But there is much useful information in Oscar Ameringer's autobiography, *If You Don't Weaken* (New York: Henry Holt and Co., 1940); Garin Burbank, *When Farmers Voted Red* (Westport, Connecticut: Greenwood Press, 1976); and James R. Green, *Grass-Roots Socialism* (Baton Rouge: Louisiana State University Press, 1978).

For the movement of different religious groups into Oklahoma see the brilliant work of Edwin Scott Gaustad, *Historical Atlas of Religion in America* (New York: Harper and Row, 1962). Sydney E. Ahlstrom's award-winning, *A Religious History of the American People*, 2 vols. (New York: Doubleday and Company, 1975), is the perfect supplement to Gaustad. For the Catholic church within Oklahoma, see Thomas Elton Brown, *Bible-Belt Catholicism* (New York: United States Catholic Historical Society, 1977). David Monaghan, ed., *One Family: One Century, A Photographic History of the Catholic Church in Oklahoma, 1875–1975* (Oklahoma City: Sooner Catholic, 1975) is surprisingly useful.

Writings by prominent immigrants are virtually nonexistent, which makes James McNamee, *Breaking the Crust of Custom* (Tulsa: privately printed, 1975) absolutely vital. This collection of sermons, essays, and letters by an activist Irish priest provides a catalogue of social issues in Oklahoma society and the Catholic church since World War II. One biography of a prominent second-generation Irishman is very useful Don Lohbeck, *Patrick J. Hurley* (Chicago: Henry Regnery Company, 1956). Also valuable in attempting to understand Oklahomans are Gordon Hines, *Alfalfa Bill* (Oklahoma City: Oklahoma Press, 1931); and the rambling William H. Murray, *Memoirs of Governor Murray and True History of Oklahoma*, 3 vols. (Boston: Meador Publishing Co., 1945).

TABLES

Table I

DECLARED DESTINATION OF BRITISH AND IRISH IMMIGRANTS ADMITTED TO UNITED STATES, 1899–1910

	Total Admitted to U.S.	Destination Indian Territory	Destination Oklahoma Territory	Total Bound for Indian and Okla. Territory	Ratio Bound for Indian and Okla. Territory
English	408,614	82	326	408	1 : 1,000
Irish	439,724	18	104	122	1 : 3,600
Scots	136,842	92	157	249	1 : 550
Welsh	20,752	12	15	27	1 : 770

Source: Computed from Dillingham Reports, Vol. I, Table 17, pp. 106–109.

Table II

STATE OF BIRTH OF WHITE POPULATION IN OKLAHOMA AND INDIAN TERRITORY COMPARED WITH THE STATE OF LAST RESIDENCE OF BRITISH & IRISH POPULATION

1890		1900	
Natives	British/Irish	Natives	British/Irish
Kansas	Kansas	Texas	Kansas
Missouri	Iowa	Missouri	Texas
Illinois	Illinois	Kansas	Iowa/Nebraska
Texas	Arkansas	Arkansas	Mississippi

Source: Data for native whites computed from Everett S. Lee, Ann R. Miller, Carol P. Brainerd and Richard A. Easterlin, *Population Redistribution and Economic Growth, United States, 1870–1950*, Vol. I, Philadelphia: The American Philosophical Society, 1957, p. 283; British and Irish data is derived from sampling of manuscript schedules of 1890 territorial census and 1900 federal census of Oklahoma Territory.

Table III

NUMBER OF OKLAHOMANS BORN IN COUNTRY INDICATED TOGETHER WITH TOTAL BRITISH AND IRISH

Year	England	Scotland	Wales	Ireland	N. Ireland	Total Britain & Ireland
1890	290	118	19	329		756
1900	1,900	737	269	1,384		4,290
1910	2,978	1,218	365	1,800		6,361
1920	2,687	1,120	319	1,321		5,447
1930	2,101	866	235	690		4,154
1940	1,323	580	125	371	262	2,506
1950	1,615	464	55	358	107	2,507
1960	1,891	380	71	203	15	2,639
1970	1,532	295	42	308	94	2,260
					83	

Source: U.S. Census Reports.

Table IV

NUMBER OF OKLAHOMANS WITH ONE OR BOTH PARENTS FROM COUNTRY INDICATED TOGETHER WITH TOTAL OF BRITISH AND IRISH PARENTAGE

Year	England	Scotland	Wales	Ireland	N. Ireland	Total Britain & Ireland
1890	651	235	40	790		1,716
1900	4,359	1,182	349	4,360		10,250
1910	2,816	1,117	354	4,509		8,787
1920	10,149	3,309	1,098	10,130		24,636
1930	11,150	3,819	1,088	7,694	2,107	25,858
1940	6,760	2,400	620	4,920	780	15,480
1950	6,360	1,755		3,910	55	12,080
1960	5,515	1,627	511	2,682	459	10,794
1970	5,702	1,410	413	2,044	249	9,818

Source: U.S. Census Reports.

Table V

BRITISH AND IRISH POPULATION OF SELECTED CITIES IN OKLAHOMA FOR SELECTED DECADES

	English	Scotch	Welsh	Irish	Total	% of Total British and Irish in Oklahoma in Selected Cities for Decade
1910						
Oklahoma City	360	97	19	202	678	
Tulsa	40	16	2	41	99	
Muskogee	69	23	7	48	147	
McAlester	71	30	22	27	150	
					1074	17
1920						
Oklahoma City	294	73	27	202	596	
Tulsa	211	64	12	41	328	
Muskogee	69	16	10	48	143	
McAlester	32	40	24	27	123	
					1190	22

1930					
Oklahoma City	317	100	17	146	580
Tulsa	279	120	18	-55	572
Muskogee	38	12	7	21	78
McAlester	25	28	22	13	88
				1318	32
1940					
Oklahoma City	221	73	12	75	381
Tulsa	177	76	21	73	347
Muskogee	19	13	1	10	43
McAlester	20	20	10	5	55
				826	34
1960					
Oklahoma City	547	90	7	89	733
Tulsa	392	91	20	62	565
				1298	49
1970					
Oklahoma City	253	53	6	55	367
Tulsa	342	98	21	51	512
				879	39

Source: U.S. Census Reports.

Table VI

PERCENT OF NATURALIZED BRITISH AND IRISH MALES AND FEMALES IN OKLAHOMA BY SELECTED AGE GROUPS

Years	Age 0–40		Age 40–60		Age 60 and above		Total Number	
	M	F	M	F	M	F	M	F
1907–19	43	40	48	50	10	0	21	2
1920–29	59	44	37	56	3	0	32	9
1930–39	22	44	41	31	36	25	58	16
1940–49	48	64	32	24	21	12	114	91
1950–59	71	85	22	11	6	3	18	115
1960–67	72	72	24	24	4	3	25	67
1968–77	52	59	44	41	4	0	25	59

Source: See note to Table IX.

Table VII

PERCENT OF NATURALIZED BRITISH AND IRISH IN OKLAHOMA BY LENGTH OF RESIDENCE IN UNITED STATES

Years	Years in U.S. 0–10		Years in U.S. 11–15		Years in U.S. 16–20		Years in U.S. 21 and over		Total Number	
	M	F	M	F	M	F	M	F	M	F
1907–19	33	50	14	0	14	0	38	50	21	2
1920–29	44	56	19	11	16	22	22	11	32	9
1930–39	24	13	5	6	10	13	60	69	58	16
1940–49	13	53	29	5	16	4	51	37	114	91
1950–59	67	78	11	10	6	0	17	12	18	115
1960–67	84	72	12	15	4	9	0	4	25	67
1968–77	56	44	24	31	12	15	8	10	25	59

Source: See note to Table IX.

Table VIII

OCCUPATIONAL STRUCTURE OF NATURALIZED BRITISH AND IRISH MALE IMMIGRANTS IN OKLAHOMA BY PERCENT

Year	Prof. & High White Collar	Low White Collar*	Skilled	Semi-Skilled	Unskilled	Total Number
1907–19	43	33	5	10	10	21
1920–29	26	48	19	3	3	31
1930–39	28	28	14	12	18	50
1940–49	21	20	8	43	8	106
1950–59	40	47	7	7	0	15
1960–67	32	44	11	5	5	18

*Farmers are included with Low White Collar.
Source: See note to Table IX.

Table IX
MARRIAGE PATTERNS OF NATURALIZED BRITISH AND IRISH IMMIGRANTS, BY PERCENT

Year	British or Irish Spouse		Spouse Born in United States		Other		Total Number	
	M	F	M	F	M	F	M	F
1907–19	39	0	50	100	11	0	18	1
1920–29	36	72	60	14	4	14	25	7
1930–39	26	27	72	36	2	37	53	11
1940–49	20	18	74	81	6	1	69	80
1950–59	43	6	44	90	13	4	16	111
1960–67	41	18	53	77	6	5	19	60
1968–77	18	7	82	93	0	0	22	54

Source: Tables VI to IX are based on all petitions for naturalization filed by British and Irish immigrants at federal courts in Oklahoma.